Kristen Schwart

Creator of *Realized Emp*

the
HEALED
EMPATH

The Highly Sensitive Person's Guide to:

Transforming
Trauma
and Anxiety

Trusting Your
Intuition

Moving from
Overwhelm to
Empowerment

FOREWORD BY KELLEY WOLF
Creator of *FLOW—Finding Love Over Worry*

FAIR WINDS

Brimming with creative inspiration, how-to projects, and useful information to enrich your everyday life, Quarto Knows is a favorite destination for those pursuing their interests and passions. Visit our site and dig deeper with our books into your area of interest: Quarto Creates, Quarto Cooks, Quarto Homes, Quarto Lives, Quarto Drives, Quarto Explores, Quarto Gifts, or Quarto Kids.

First Published in 2022 by Fair Winds Press, an imprint of The Quarto Group, 100 Cummings Center, Suite 265-D, Beverly, MA 01915, USA.
T (978) 282-9590 F (978) 283-2742 QuartoKnows.com

Fair Winds Press titles are also available at discount for retail, wholesale, promotional, and bulk purchase. For details, contact the Special Sales Manager by email at specialsales@quarto.com or by mail at The Quarto Group, Attn: Special Sales Manager, 100 Cummings Center, Suite 265-D, Beverly, MA 01915, USA.

26 25 24 23 22   1 2 3 4 5

ISBN: 978-0-7603-7173-2

Digital edition published in 2022

eISBN: 978-0-7603-7174-9

Library of Congress Cataloging-in-Publication Data

Names: Schwartz, Kristen, author.
Title: The healed empath / Kristen Schwartz.
Description: Beverly, MA : Fair Winds Press, an imprint of The Quarto
  Group, 2021. | Includes index. | Summary: "Drawing from neuroscience,
  psychology, and spirituality, The Healed Empath shows empaths and highly
  sensitive individuals practical techniques for managing their emotions
  and reclaiming their boundaries and sense of personal power"-- Provided
  by publisher.
Identifiers: LCCN 2021029159 (print) | LCCN 2021029160 (ebook) | ISBN
  9780760371732 (trade paperback) | ISBN 9780760371749 (ebook)
Subjects: LCSH: Empathy. | Sensitivity (Personality trait) | Boundaries
  (Psychology)
Classification: LCC BF575.E55 S43 2021 (print) | LCC BF575.E55 (ebook) |
  DDC 152.4/1--dc23
LC record available at https://lccn.loc.gov/2021029159
LC ebook record available at https://lccn.loc.gov/2021029160

Design, page layout, and illustration: Tanya Jacobson, jcbsn.co

Printed in China

For my courageous inner-child,
thank you for paving the way.
I hear you, I see you,
I feel you, I love you,
I got you.

CONTENTS

Part I

A Foundation

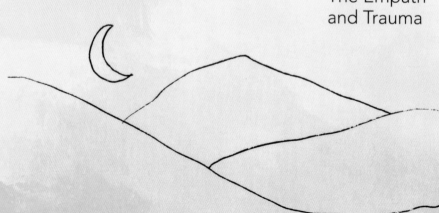

Part II

The Healed Empath

Foreword

BY KELLEY WOLF, Author and founder of *FLOW—Finding Love Over Worry*

I live by this deeply held belief: When we learn, we must teach. This is what Kristen has done for all of us in *The Healed Empath*. *The Healed Empath* is a master class for empaths and those desiring profound knowledge of the human condition in all its beautiful complexities.

I believe Kristen did not just learn this information by reading books, although she did that. She also learned from living the life of an empath. She brings the kind of knowledge that can only come from a person who has traveled the complicated road of feeling on a level that defies ordinary understanding.

Kristen and I are colleagues, and we found each other through mutual respect for each other's work. Each time I read Kristen's words, I shake my head, "How does she know?" "Is she inside my head?" I, too, am an empath; and my journey, like Kristen's, was peppered with the complex nature of this profound gift.

One of the most striking moments I had while reading *The Healed Empath* was in the intuition sections. As an empath, you can feel people's emotions. When you are young, this can disrupt your ability to tap into what you think is your intuition. Is it mine, or is it being filtered through another? Learning to trust one's instinct is one of the greatest gifts we could receive, especially as an empath.

In chapter 9, Kristen writes, "An empath's intuition is one of their best assets, and reconnecting to it can alter the trajectory of their lives. When empaths trust themselves, they open up to unlimited possibilities and experiencing the life they were born to live."

These words were a revelation—a salve to my spirit. Imagine your intuition as a grandmother from your life. Imagine the day you drive down her familiar road, take the last turn toward the house, and see her standing on the porch, waving. When you embrace, or should I say integrate, the powers of an empath with their intuition, it is like a homecoming—calm, faithful, nourishing, and familiar.

I can boldly say that an empath is often the one to put their needs last. When you can feel the gravity of others' emotions, I dare say, it is easier to focus on them than your own needs. This becomes a sick habit until you become ill.

I wish I would have had this book ten years ago when my body gave way to illness after collecting others' needs and emotions. I remember walking into a party when I was first married, and I said to my husband, "I need to leave; I can feel everyone, and it's not good." He looked at me with confusion. I did not understand what to do with this information and how to care for myself. And that night, like every other, I stayed at the party and drank too much to block the empathic intake. Either way, I took it until my body finally shut down.

This book could save you from experiencing the pitfalls many of us faced. I get it; the word *boundary* has become a catchphrase, often without clarification.

In chapter 7, Kristen writes, "Empaths can feel all that they feel and perceive all that they perceive and thrive without other people changing. What we sense does not obligate us to entangle ourselves with it. We are not bound to heal or repair anything outside of ourselves. We may attempt to fix others, but we are not obligated. Our obligation in this life is to heal ourselves. When we spend the bulk of our energy healing and fixing others and neglect ourselves, we pay a substantial price."

But hear me now: If you are an empath or highly sensitive person (HSP), or frankly any human that feels deeply, learning to hold your boundaries with others' emotions and problems could save *your* life!

I hope I said that loud enough, and I hope you will have your highlighter ready for chapter 7. I highlighted the whole chapter. I am 44 years old, and I have a thriving career as a writer, podcaster, and life coach. I am a mother of three and a wife to a wonderful man. Let me say it this way: My life is full. I often have no choice but to interact. Whether it is a school bake sale or a red-carpet event (my husband is an actor), I am always surrounded by people. If I do not learn how to execute my boundaries, I can become ill and tired; I can barely function. I once almost crumbled on a red carpet because I could feel the energy of the many photographers. I could feel the excitement of some, and I could feel the disdain of others. I was so plugged into the cascade of feelings, I could hardly stand still and smile.

Kristen sent me a draft of her book before anyone could buy it. I knew the importance of keeping it safe, and I held that responsibility close to my heart. As I started reading, I suddenly felt the urge to share the magic of this book. I decided to list all the people I would buy the book for; my list kept growing and growing. I do not believe each person on my list is a true empath, but I know each person will find immense value in these pages. You will see. Each chapter brings new permission to break the chains of trauma and anxiety and step into something truly magical—your freedom.

Thank you, Kristen, for the time and care you have given to these words. They will change lives. They have changed mine.

NAVIGATING
THIS BOOK

Empath, think of this book as a road sign on your journey, kindly pointing you to bumps in the road, turns, and the rest stops necessary to care for your unique needs.

You, empath, are an incredible soul who, when properly cared for, has the potential to change the world. Tapping into the highest version of yourself requires an understanding of what holds you back. What fears, beliefs, and past pain keep you from stepping into your power, and what tools can provide a detour around your roadblocks? Our trip together will remind us that our sensitivity and our intuitive nature are gifts. You will remember that it is okay to be different and that you are not alone.

It is essential to remember that "healed" does not mean arriving at a final destination. In this book's context, "healed" refers to a mindset that embraces a daily commitment to an empath's well-being. A healed empath does not escape nor arrive beyond difficulty or pain. A healed empath honors that light comes with shadow, and when the empath experiences a moment of shadow, they will remember the wholeness of who they are and venture further into their potential. A healed empath knows that life has difficulties and they are equipped with the tools, compassion, grace, and self-commitment to navigate the winding road.

Does traveling this road seem like a towering endeavor? It is understandable if it does, but you were born to venture into your absolute potential. I do not believe in consequences. You are here for a reason. You can do hard things. You are ready.

To get the most out of this book, let us review some things that, when implemented, create a better reading experience for you.

- **Take care of yourself.** Taking care of your needs as an empath is a recurring theme throughout this book. Empaths are their best selves when they are aware of their needs and taking steps to meet them.

- **Be open to new ideas.** Take what resonates and leave the rest. When we are evolving and healing, we are open to the messages that match your consciousness level. It is okay if some information does not apply. That message is not for you; it is for someone else. The messages meant for you will always find you if you are open to receiving.

- **Be easy on yourself.** Always be kind and compassionate to you. Forgive yourself. Be willing to see your strengths in the things you consider your weaknesses.

- **Practice thought awareness.** Thought awareness is a powerful way to fast-track healing. When we practice noticing our thoughts, we will start to see our limited beliefs and behavior patterns that block your growth and healing.

If you picked up this book because you, like me, feel everything, you are not alone. We can feel the pain, fear, sadness, and joy of people all around us; and we sense we are here for a grand purpose. Fellow empath, I am glad you are here. Let us take this journey together and venture into what it means to be a fully realized empath— protected, awakened, empowered, and free.

Part I

A FOUNDATION

We live in a world that avoids pain, suppresses feelings, and points outside of itself to bypass the arduous work of healing. We all do it. My hope for us is that we notice our urge to point outside ourselves and allow it to transform into an invitation to heal. When we embrace our pain and see how avoiding our feelings affects our daily experience, we peel away the layers that hold us apart from our highest self.

The empath who heals themselves is less affected by the swirling energy around them. The energy that is yours becomes apparent. You prioritize your needs without regret, and you give from your overfill instead of draining your reserve. A healed empath realizes that their empathic gifts are deserving of the effort it requires to change. The healed empath recognizes that their lifestyle equates to their welfare, and self-care is how they step into their purpose.

You, empath, are a gift; and the world needs the whole of who you are. You are not too sensitive or too much, and your experiences and feelings are valid. You are what this aching planet needs. Do not let anyone, including yourself, tell you any different.

The world needs more people honoring how they feel, taking accountability for their wellbeing, and embracing differences. The change we crave begins with us; it starts by accepting, caring, and nurturing all of who we are. When we take accountability for our energy, we can show up in a world starving for compassion and be the light we came here to be.

ch 1 WHO IS THE EMPATH?

Empaths feel the pain of others—quite literally.

Being an empath is like having six senses rather than five. Other people are not aware that empaths can sense others' emotions even without seeing overt expressions of them. They can notice another's anger, grief, or joy when that person does not verbalize it.

I realized I was an empath many years ago. Most of my life, my emotional world kept me in constant torment. Life felt difficult. Filtering the magnitude of what I felt seemed an unrelenting task. As I grew older and experienced my moments of personal trauma, it began to feel impossible to distinguish my feelings about what was happening to me versus the pain I was picking up from others. I started internalizing everything I experienced, and in hindsight, I see that I equated my overwhelm as proof I was fundamentally flawed. Eventually, my experiences of trauma, which needed compassion and loving attention, were drowned by the unrelenting pain and suffering of the world around me.

I became desperate to feel something other than pain, confusion, and rejection. The idea of permanent escape became enticing. I wanted the pain to stop; I wanted to feel less around others. I wanted a break from the constant input; I wanted to feel safe sharing what I was going through. I began believing life and those in it were a threat to my peace, and I developed coping mechanisms to protect myself. To survive my feelings and experiences, I disconnected from my intuition, I stopped paying attention to my body's cues, and I followed other people's emotions, opinions, and expectations. I bought into the falsehood that I was innately flawed and could not trust what I felt. I thought I was broken in some way and destined to suffer; hiding was the only option. For most of my life, I did what I believed would dull the pain and mute the energy—like morphing myself to fit the environment and hiding my feelings. I did what I thought would avoid upset in them and me.

I survived by ignoring what I felt until I could not. I exhausted all means to avoid and numb out input. I chased symptoms like low self-worth, emotional eating, and anxiety. I attempted to alter the symptoms through diets, fitness, medication, and relationship changes.

I survived this way until the day I met myself in a dark corner of a room with no means of escape. On that day, I began looking for answers, not escaping into others' words but looking for answers deep within myself. I started pulling back from the world around me, not to isolate out of fear but to quiet the feedback. As I stopped listening, I began to hear.

I wondered why I was profoundly affected by other people's emotions. I questioned whether there was something defective about me. I was too sensitive and overly emotional. Negative energy did not affect other people how it affected me; others did not pick up what I noticed or felt. Fear, judgment, and sadness and the negative energy I noticed from other people silently accumulated each day. Added to the trauma I had experienced, life had become so overwhelming that my chest felt as if it had a fifty-pound weight on it, leaving me in constant physical pain.

As I began diving deeper into myself, I asked questions like:

* *Why do I feel the energy under the words?*
* *Why do I feel physically drained and anxious in crowds?*
* *Why do I experience shifting energy in conversations?*
* *Why does negativity make me feel the need to retreat?*
* *Why does it take me weeks to recover from holidays and busy vacations?*
* *Why does it seem that I cannot thrive in our society like most people?*

It was questions like these that led me to see others experiencing life as I do. I began to see people who felt overwhelmed in public places or around crowds. I saw women who took on others' emotions as their own and men who "know" before they are told. I found others who feel fatigued and need alone time to recharge. Life began to make more sense.

"

I wondered why I was profoundly affected by other people's emotions. I believed there was something innately defective about me.

What is an Empath?

An empath is someone who can sense the experiences and feelings of others. To understand empaths, one must look at empathy and the brain structures that enable people to feel sorrow when their friends and family are sad. Neurons are the cells in our brain that receive messages from the body and the sense organs. Our sense organs respond to external stimuli and relay messages to our nervous system. The sense organs include our eyes, ears, and skin.

Whenever the body experiences something, a message will flash through the nervous system to the brain, where neurons light up in response. Mirror neurons, scientists believe, are the vehicle for empathy, lighting up in response to seeing others' experiences. Mirror neurons, or what the American Psychology Association calls the mind's mirror, activate in our brain, allowing humans to connect to what others are experiencing. Highly sensitive people have been shown to have an increased amount of mirror neurons, which aid in feeling the emotions of others.

Empaths, it is believed, have highly advanced mirror neurons that respond to very subtle and almost imperceptible signals that let them sense others' emotions so strongly that they feel a similar emotion. Empaths, in short, can feel what everyone else feels before it is communicated.

HIGHLY SENSITIVE PEOPLE VS. EMPATHS

Most empaths are highly sensitive people (HSPs), but not all HSPs are empaths. HSPs share many traits with empaths, qualities such as being easily overwhelmed by sensory input, being affected by others' moods, being easily startled by loud noises, being negatively affected by violent content, and having an easily frazzled nervous system. HSPs, like empaths, are hyper-aware of others' emotional states and the subtle nuances around them.

By contrast, empaths have one defining trait: the ability to intuit and feel others' emotions. HSPs may sympathize with others' pain, but they will not feel it as though it is their pain. Watching a conversation between an empath and another

person can be a revelation, as the emotions passing over the face and showing in the speaker's body language will be mirrored in the empath's face and body. This happens spontaneously and is in no way an attempt to mock or copy the speaker. It is the result of the empath's mirror neurons receiving the emotions so strongly that they experience what the speaker is feeling.

Ask yourself this question to help you decipher whether you are an empath or an HSP: **Am I experiencing their state of being, or am I simply particularly good at recognizing how they feel?**

Understanding how you experience the world is essential in knowing how to care for our sensitive selves. Elaine Aron, Ph.D., the author of *The Highly Sensitive Person*, estimates in her research that only 15 to 20 percent of the world's population is highly sensitive. This detail is relevant in understanding why empaths and HSPs can suffer. Most of us grew up with life modeled by those who are not highly sensitive. It is no wonder that good portions of empaths and HSPs are not sure how to best care for their sensitivity.

IF I FEEL EMPATHY, AM I AN EMPATH?

An empath's experience is not to be confused with the feeling of empathy. Being an empath is more emotionally intense than most can understand. Someone may feel empathy when a friend or a stranger is suffering, and they may feel sorrow, cry, or feel ill on their behalf; but they do not experience the depth of emotion that the other person is feeling in the way that an empath does. It is the difference between watching a television show and sitting in the front row of an immersive theatre performance—and even that analogy may be an understatement. When empaths witness what occurs in others, it stimulates the brain's visual cortex, which is the part of the brain that processes visual information. It also enables our emotions and sensations to make us feel similar ways.

Another key difference is that, when in a crowd, empaths are unable to shut themselves off emotionally and energetically from the people surrounding them. An empath can find public outings overwhelming, as they are bombarded with emotions and feelings from everyone around them. Feeling so much can be scary (such as driving during morning rush hour when commuters are intensely determined to get where they need to be), or it can be exhilarating (experiencing a happy horde of concert fans screaming for their favorite artist). Empaths feel everything to the maximum, and without understanding how to let go of the more intense feelings, an empath can question their worthiness and purpose.

EMPATHY VS. SYMPATHY

Empathy differs from sympathy.

Sympathy is *feeling sorry for another*, while **empathy** attempts to *understand how it feels for that person.*

Feeling sorry for someone is not beneficial to a relationship, whereas empathy communicates that we genuinely understand what they are going through. Empathy is perception. When you perceive what someone is experiencing and communicate that back to that person, it makes the other person feel understood, deepening the connection.

Perception without being able to communicate your understanding is ineffective and does not build an empathic connection. For example, let us say you are watching an emotional movie and become involved in a character and feel a powerful bond with them. You can perceive that, but you cannot communicate back to the actor. Therefore, the empathy cycle is incomplete.

Empathic Prism

To some extent, all humans can empathize with others; to what degree depends on the individual. Empaths feel empathy to the greatest extent. There are many empathy variations, like cognitive (understanding how someone feels) and emotional (the sharing in another's feelings). Like other emotions, empathy can be experienced on various levels.

According to Truax and Carkhuff's 1967 Communication Scale, there are five levels of empathy.

- LEVEL 1 / low (little or no awareness of feelings)
- LEVEL 2 / moderately low level (minimum realization)
- LEVEL 3 / a reciprocal level of empathic response (mirrored at a similar level)
- LEVEL 4 / reasonably high empathic response (ability to reflect the real and underlying feeling)
- LEVEL 5 / an elevated level of empathic response (a precise reflection of sentiment, plus underlying feelings in greater depth)

Empaths would be considered a level 5 on the above list, though, due to lack of scientific data, empaths may experience empathy on a level not represented on this list.

WHAT IS IT LIKE BEING AN EMPATH?

Is being an empath and experiencing life as one a positive or a negative? It is dependent on how you are living it. With everything in life, there are difficulties. Some of our greatest strengths can turn into our most significant weaknesses if we are not conscious of our intentions and living within healthy boundaries.

One of my extraordinary strengths is taking immediate action without procrastination, clarifying aspirations, and taking the necessary steps to manifest my vision. Through self-awareness, I know emotional trauma forged this strength; it was born from the false belief that I am fundamentally flawed and need to prove myself through doing. Because trauma shaped this strength, I know it can quickly become a weakness if I am not approaching things with conscious consideration.

As I draft this book, it feels natural to sit down and get the work done each day. I am mindful of my time and thoughts, and I set necessary boundaries (two-hour writing stints, following my body's cue). I can easily slip into pushing myself to do more at the detriment of my physical and mental health if I am not watching my thoughts and listening to my body. Empaths can thrive, and some can barely survive. I have found what differentiates the two is how they care for themselves and how willing they are to change their lifestyle to cater to their sensitive needs.

How an empath cares for their unique needs can alter their experience positively and independent of the outside world, creating a life whose foundation is rich in self-acceptance and love.

Are You An Empath?

Are you wondering if you are an empath? I am a firm believer in looking within to answer that question. As we heal from our past and release our self-limiting beliefs, we become increasingly aware of the parts of ourselves we did not notice before. When I began to wonder if I was an empath, it helped to find resources like books, quizzes, and social media groups. I utilized the resources for clarity about my traits versus the traits of an empath. Below you will find a quiz; it can help you gain insight into your empathic abilities. Please remember a few questions cannot tell you who you are. That is an inside job.

EMPATH QUIZ

Answer the questions and count the number of Yes.

- Do strangers often over-share their life with you?
- Do you need lots of alone time to recharge?
- Are you deeply connected to nature?
- Do you need to avoid violent content and movies?
- Have you been told you are too sensitive?
- Do you get overwhelmed in crowds or at significant events?
- Is your intuition powerful, though you may not always trust it?
- Do you feel weighed down by emotions when around someone who is suffering?
- Is sleep critical to you (more than most)?
- Do you sometimes prioritize others' wellness over your own?

Calculate your yes responses. If you received seven to ten, you might be an empath.

Hopefully, whether you are an empath is becoming more transparent. Did you know that empaths can vary in type and differ in personality style?

Introverts, Extroverts, and the Empath

Though it may seem that empaths are introverted, not all empaths are introverts. An introvert is someone whose energy drains in social situations—the brain of an introvert processes dopamine differently. Dopamine is a neurotransmitter in the body. Our body makes dopamine and shares it with the nervous system. Dopamine plays a role in feeling pleasure. The introvert's "reward" center activates in scenarios centered on calm, quiet reflection, whereas an extrovert's "reward" center aligns with more social and outwardly energetic situations.

Introverts need time alone to recharge their energy; they fill up their energy from within, not through other people. Introverts are hyper-aware of their inner world and can thrive in solitude. On the contrary, extroverts fill their energy around others; they are more outspoken and outgoing and thrive in social situations.

EMPATHS CAN BE INTROVERTED OR EXTROVERTED

Extroverted empaths can crave a lot of human connection but still feel drained afterward. They can thrive in various personal relationships with less overwhelm. They reenergize around others and need alone time, too. Extroverted empaths love to understand people on a deeper level, just like the introverted empath. It is important to note that being introverted or extroverted can be something we are born with, and sometimes we can appear timid when we struggle internally, do not feel safe, or are tired. We can also appear to be more extroverted when we are uncomfortable or nervous or have had too much coffee.

My point is that we are humans, and humans do not usually fit into tidy boxes. Notice and honor your tendencies and, at the same time, leave space to surprise yourself.

EMPATH TYPES

We are all unique intuitive beings, and how we experience the world is primarily affected by our thoughts about our past, our unhealed pain, and our temperament. For empaths, their type accounts for their individuality, too.

Emotional Empath

One of the more common types of empaths is an emotional empath. The emotional empath can notice and even take on the emotions of others. Emotional empaths are particularly susceptible to stronger, more negative energy and may feel drained around prolonged negativity.

Physical Empath

Like emotional empaths, a physical empath notices the experiences of others; but here, it is physical symptoms they manifest rather than emotional ones. A physical empath can feel the pain and ailments in their body that another person is experiencing.

Intuitive Empath

An intuitive empath's intuition is incredibly strong, and they can notice what other people are feeling and thinking and may even pick up lower moods and stress in a room.

Plant/Animal/Earth Empath

The finely attuned earth/planet empath feels the needs of plants, animals, and the planet. They tune into the needs and suffering of creatures around them and sense the planet's imbalances. For instance, an earth empath could feel sensations such as anxiety, heaviness in the chest, or even sadness when a catastrophic earthquake was impending.

Empaths exist across a full array of sensitivities and possibilities; their experience is as unique as the universe itself. Many resonate with multiple types, and some will resonate with one. They are distinct and not meant to fit into boxes. They can take their personal experience, explore their abilities, and develop their unique gifts.

ARE EMPATHS BORN OR CREATED?

Is being an empath something we are born into, or are we shaped into one through suffering or other conditioning? Does genetics pass down empathic traits? Are they part of our temperament? Can we become highly sensitive people due to trauma?

As I navigated my healing journey and worked with many sensitive souls, I realized there are numerous explanations of how one becomes an empath.

Possibility 1: Temperament. This became clear after the birth of my babies. Some of us enter the world with more sensitivity—it is a natural temperament present at birth. I witnessed it myself when my children came out of the womb. These babies were more responsive to light, smells, touch, movement, temperature, and sound. These babies appeared to be empaths from the start. If nurtured, these babies can confidently grow into who they are.

Possibility 2: Our Genes. Like temperament, our parents may genetically transfer our level of empathy. In 2018, scientists from the University of Cambridge worked with genetics company 23andMe and a team of international scientists, and they found how empathetic we are is partly due to our genetics (e.g., highly sensitive children may have a highly sensitive parent or grandparent). If sensitive traits are nurtured, we become more aware and accepting of who we are.

Possibility 3: Trauma. Trauma, or what I call experiences that our nervous system cannot naturally process, can modify our sensitivity levels. Many empaths I work with share traumatic events that altered how they process and internalize the world around them. Trauma can create a hyper-aware state that can wear down a person's nervous system, making the person's hyper-aware state a new normal.

No matter how the empath came to be, one thing is for sure: Empaths connect deeply to the world around them. We are not like most of the planet; therefore, caring for ourselves must be different, too.

"

Empaths exist across a full array
of sensitivities and possibilities;
their experience is as unique as
the universe itself.

ARE EMPATHS REAL?

It may concern some that science lacks research on why "empaths" experience the world as they do. You may hear, read, or have someone tell you being an empath is not real. Here is what I say to those concerns: Everything once was not in a scientific journal; everything once was not discovered or understood. What matters most is your understanding of yourself and your willingness to stand confidently in your unique interpretation of the world.

The word *empath* is, in fact, a label. Take the title away and you have individual humans interpreting their experience of the world around them. Research is trending positively toward humans with increased sensitivity, heightened awareness, and the brains' differences in such individuals. In decades prior, generations were less likely to speak about things that made them different. Modern medicine revolves around a model that diagnoses ailments instead of fostering whole health. We live in an age when showing our differences is becoming better received and embracing our diversity feels safer.

All humans are intuitive beings; we are all empaths to some extent. History shows that humans tend to denounce what they do not understand or experience themselves. Knowing this, I hope you will continue to explore your empathic gifts, resist the urge to explain yourself to those committed to misunderstanding you, and feel empowered to stand in the growing knowledge of who you are.

Before I truly understood who I was and why I experienced the world as I did, I spent most of my time in overwhelm. I thought my strengths were weaknesses and believed my weaknesses were proof of my unworthiness. My innate ability to perceive more deeply made me different; my feelings made others uncomfortable, which created a disconnection.

I did not know who I was or why I mattered. I could not turn off how the world felt, but I could distract myself, pretend it was fine, please others to minimize upset, and avoid when it became too much. The limiting beliefs I developed and my unhealthy coping mechanisms held me apart from my greatest strength for two-thirds of my life. And it would be my awareness of this that set me free.

As we have learned, empaths exist across a broad spectrum of personality traits, sensitivities, and physical experiences. There is not one box an empath can fit in. It is expected that a newly realized empath would be unclear about their unique sensitivities and unsure on steps to nourish them. However, as you become familiar with your emotional reality, you will find that your empathic gifts are yearning to be tuned into and nurtured.

One way to encourage your empathic skills is by reacquainting yourself with your most significant strengths, for example, by sorting through our common struggles.

ch 2 THE EMPATH, STRUGGLES, AND STRENGTHS

From an early age, I wanted to learn about the human mind.

By thirteen, I was adamant about a career in psychology. What guided me to this decision was not an interest in the human brain or a longing to heal others. What fed this decision was a desire to understand me and grasp why people caused such pain. I thought if I received the degrees, I could explain why life felt as it did. If I examined all there was about the human psyche, there was a chance my experience would change.

I was an intuitive, profoundly feeling child. I remember struggling to manage all that I witnessed, experienced, and felt. I recall questioning if my experience was normal, and if it was, why did everyone else handle it so well? By thirteen, I had endured my share of trauma. In the third grade, my teacher sexually groomed three of his students, including myself, eventually leading to inappropriate talk and touch. I fearfully watched his career continue as he became a fifth-grade teacher as I ascended into fifth grade. Schoolmates relentlessly bullied me through elementary and middle school, leading me at twelve to write a desperate letter to the principal, stating I could not go on, begging him to make it stop.

29

These experiences are traumatic for anyone to endure, and making it especially damning was my awareness of how everyone else felt. I felt the fear, frustration, and need for an unhealthy connection from my third-grade teacher. I felt the adults' guilt, anxiety, and fear when the topic came up, and I felt my bullying classmates' self-doubt and desire to fit in. What was I to do with what I felt? Was I to prioritize my pain over theirs? Was I safe to ask for help when my problem caused others pain? How could I focus on my needs when the needs of others felt just as specific? I had endured so much pain at others' hands; if I focus on helping them, will that decrease the chance people will hurt me again? How could feeling everything at this level be a positive thing? How could my existence be what God intended? This time in my life was when I began thinking my strengths were weaknesses and started focusing on making others feel better, hoping to earn myself a moment of peace.

My story will be different from yours, but I have found most empaths do share one experience: Most of us grow up without understanding why we are different. We do not know how to care for our unique needs, and we use our differences as proof that we are fundamentally flawed and search for ways to ease our pain. We develop coping mechanisms hoping to alleviate struggle, but on the contrary, we create more challenges for ourselves. Here are common strains an empath may experience.

Struggles

LOW SELF-ESTEEM

Empaths can be prone to low self-esteem. Being unlike most of the world, they may judge themselves against non-empaths. It is less about comparing monetary possessions or physical attributes and more about the desire to release themselves from a world they feel and observe. And being that they are unlike most of the world, the world may not accept them.

It is as if they walk around life taking in all the subtle hints of pain and suffering, and they are looking at people around them and saying, "Are you guys seeing this?," then they realize the answer is mostly a resounding no. Unlike empaths, most people have natural energetic boundaries. When two such people approach each other for a conversation, they will notice typical body language cues and tap into their empathy if the discussion turns sad. Still, those with specific energetic boundaries will not feel the energy behind the forced smile; they will not sense the feelings under the small talk. When the discussion is over, these two people walk away without remnants of their brief time together.

On the other hand, the empath's energetic field is open and sensitive to all imbalances within another, even if the irregularities are not communicated. It is as if empaths have antennas that absorb all disturbing signals, and until we understand why this is occurring, we take all that we feel into our bodies and make it our responsibility. We believe we are the reason this person is feeling bad, that we are making this person uncomfortable; and after time, our self-trust and self-worth can plummet. We do not have an explanation for everything we feel, and it seems the only explanation is something is wrong with us.

SHAME

Shame is commonly defined as an intense negative emotion characterized by the perception of a global devaluation of oneself. Empaths can struggle with shame. When they hold shame, they believe that they are flawed and undeserving of unconditional love and acceptance. Shame sounds like "I should have scored higher on that test; I'm an idiot." Guilt sounds like "I was capable of scoring higher on that test; I should have studied more."

Empaths can develop personal shame by hearing comments suggesting you are too sensitive: "Why do you cry so much?" "It is not that big of a deal." "Get over it." These statements communicate one is too much or not enough. When comments like these recur over the years, they become a person's inner voice and deeply impact self-worth. When an empath feels shame toward their greatest strength, it becomes difficult to thrive and enjoy one's life.

CODEPENDENCY

Due to our former experiences, many empaths do not develop a solid understanding of what makes us unique. To fit in, we acquire a practice of searching outside ourselves for validation and a sense of worthiness. Because we are hyper-aware of others' emotional states, we can become people-pleasers, hoping if we help, they will see our worth—in turn, meeting our inner need for validation.

An empath with codependent tendencies will have relationships focusing on the other person, providing us with what we lack internally rather than mutual vulnerability, sharing, and healthy boundaries. When we think we are broken and believe we cannot meet our needs, we put that responsibility onto others. Codependency can show up as external focusing, modeling our attitudes and behaviors from circumstances outside ourselves or self-sacrifice, consistently neglecting our needs to focus on others' needs. Codependency can also look like emotional suppression, little self-awareness of our personal needs, and interpersonal friction, engaging in a relationship cultivating a lack of self-expression.

With codependency, loving others is not the issue. It is the inability to love the self that causes the dysfunction.

ANXIETY

The upside of being an empath is that they profoundly feel all the positive and nourishing energy in the world. The downside is that empaths become fatigued, anxious, and overwhelmed from sensory overload. Anxiety is the potent, excessive, and incessant worry about everyday situations. When an empath learns that their sensitivity isn't appreciated, welcome, or is worthy of ridicule, empaths assume they are not safe being themselves.

Anxiety remains a go-to state—for me, when I am overstimulated, overly tired, or unaware of my thoughts. I was in a state of overwhelm for many years, and anxiety was a regular occurrence. Even now, I must be mindful of my body and feel for its cues that communicate when care is required. When empaths do not know how to process and release what they perceive, they become afraid of what they will feel next. In short, they fear the very thing that makes them who they are—sensitive, intuitive, feeling beings.

RESENTMENT

A boundary awareness exercise I do with my clients is to list all the resentment they hold and for whom they hold it. This simple exercise illuminates the areas and relationships in their life that require boundaries. Lack of boundaries is one of the main reasons empaths have resentment; the other is lack of self-acceptance. Let me explain. An unidentified empath learns through experience that being in the presence of others can feel uncomfortable; the empath feels the heaviness, doubt, judgment, fear, and the good stuff, too. It is relentless.

The empath does not know why these feelings are so overwhelming, does not question the feelings, and assumes they must be self-managed. Imagine every person you approach gives you a forty-pound (18.1 kg) weight and you have no choice but to carry them everywhere you go. The option to give them back is not there, and the idea of setting them down and walking away does not seem feasible.

Bearing the expanding weight is what it is like for an empath before boundaries. The load becomes too heavy to carry, and its weight overshadows any personal needs the empath may have. This is the birthplace of resentment. Empaths can believe there is no choice in the energy they experience and begin resenting those whose energy they still shoulder and avoid new acquaintances based on how they feel around them. The resentment builds from a desire to lighten their load. According to an article in the *International Journal of Research Studies in Psychology*, "Self-acceptance is the very foundation of one's identity before developing other areas of personal well-being."

Empaths may not know they can sense heavy energy without absorbing it or feel safe without others needing to change. This leads us to another reason empaths can hold resentment. Highly sensitive people tend to be extremely hard on themselves, saying things like "I should be able to handle this." Many empaths believe if they get everything perfect, they will feel better. Lack of self-acceptance slithers into the nonacceptance of others. "If only I could change, my life would feel better"; this becomes "If only they'd change, my life would feel better."

The tendency to believe that others' change determines our happiness invites our infringement of others' boundaries. An empath can develop a habit of inserting themselves into others' lives, hoping to earn a sense of safety. Freeing ourselves from resentment begins with forgiving ourselves and forgiving others, then moving forward, taking full responsibility for our boundaries.

COPING MECHANISMS

Before I could make sense of my experience, I felt overwhelmed and defeated. I witnessed others handling life pretty well. I assumed they were experiencing what I was, so I thought I was missing something. To survive the pain that comes from believing the core of who we are is the worst of who we are, we develop coping mechanisms. Coping mechanisms are how our minds survive the stress of believing we are not safe being ourselves. Empaths are not alone in developing defense mechanisms. Coping mechanisms are a normal part of human development. Sigmund Freud said, "Defense mechanisms are psychological strategies that are unconsciously used to protect a person from anxiety arising from unacceptable thoughts or feelings." As the feeling of not being safe in my body grew, I developed coping mechanisms that, after working with empaths, appear to be commonly shared.

Pretend You Do Not Feel Anything

Yes, empaths sense when things are off; and yes, an empath is capable of speaking truth into an imbalance that, if open to it, a person(s) can benefit. But many will not be open to hearing the truth. Before, I understood that people hear what they were ready to receive; and too much truth is threatening. I inserted truth whenever I felt somebody suffering.

Twenty-two years ago, spending time with my husband's (then boyfriend) friends, I witnessed one of his friends make disparaging comments about his pregnant girlfriend. The young woman awkwardly smiled, attempting to play it off as if she did not care, but I felt everything under the smile. As the young men left the table, I turned to her and said, "You're beautiful pregnant; don't believe anything he says to you." Within thirty minutes, she told her boyfriend; and within minutes, I was called names, screamed at, and shunned by the men, including my husband's brother. This emotional abuse would continue for many years from this group of men.

I assumed all those who suffer welcomed truth and feeling better, and I thought the fast track to their relief was sharing that I witnessed their pain. In this situation, I could feel her feelings, I offered compassion and love, and I was labeled a "female dog" and identified as a threat to how these men operated—and the girlfriend sat back and watched. I learned to keep quiet even though the urge to share, comfort those in pain, and speak truth to behavior that is hurting others burned through my soul. I realized feeling for others meant torment and abuse for me.

Be the Fixer

Empaths can read the energy in the room, and without healthy boundaries, they absorb the energy, emotions, thoughts, and beliefs of those around them. This can be an overwhelming experience, especially when they do not know how to manage the enormity of what they feel. They learn from an early age that they could not control what they were feeling, so it is best to fix what others felt to lighten their load. Hoping to lighten their load can show up as people-pleasing and assuming the role as the fixer.

Possibly you mastered the art of homing in on others' immense feelings to avoid sitting with your feelings. Maybe you lost connection to what makes you happy because you have been focusing on their happiness for so long. In fact, you may have felt like you do not have much of an identity of your own because you are so immersed in the wants and needs of others. What I did not learn until much later is by focusing on pleasing them, I was not living my life for me. The more I pleased, the more I lost who I was and the deeper into despair I fell.

Do Not Get Too Close or You Will Get Hurt

Let me premise this with self-awareness. I understand my being bullied for many years affected my attachment style, and coping mechanisms can have multiple explanations based on the trauma we endure. As an empath, playing it safe can equate to feeling less. Playing it safe can look like codependent relationships where the other person needs you, so you are safe from abandonment; or it can be befriending those who are emotionally unavailable so you can stay unavailable, too. We can put up walls to stem off feeling love and loss at its full intensity. We may protect ourselves from showing our feelings' depth because we learned most are not comfortable with depth.

"

What I did not learn until
much later is by focusing
on pleasing them, I was not
living my life for me.

I learned that getting close meant I would notice discrepancies and incongruences within them, imbalances they may not be ready to share; and to me, that equated to a threat and led to my distrust. I look back over my life and see how I kept people at a distance, thinking the next relationship would be different. Maybe I'd feel less around the next person; perhaps I could let my guard down in a future relationship where the other person is safer. I was not ready to accept that all people have pain, struggle, and at times incongruences. I did not understand my empathic tendencies or see the disempowering beliefs I had adopted and the coping behaviors I used to protect myself.

Focus on "Fixing" External "Flaws"

As I have mentioned before, it is prevalent for humans to change their outside world if they do not believe changing their inner world is an option. Society reinforces this message: It is in advertising, selling the story of a happy woman who just shopped at a particular store; on the news in the narrative that says to think this way to be worthy of inclusion; and in unaware parents who reinforce it by putting their children on diets, modeling that fitting in begins with altering your body.

Young empaths can feel helpless, managing the depth and frequency of their feelings. Looking back at that time, I envision a young girl with her palms up, arms stretched out in front of her. Her arms are full of hers and others' feelings. She looks around with her arms stretched out, hoping that others will see what she has and offer support. Instead, she receives shoulder shrugs, rolled eyes, and turned backs. In hindsight, I understand the young girl was searching for safety and commonality in a world that did not experience life as I did. Not finding that commonality and safety would have a profound impact on me for many years to come.

Concluding that I could not manage my inner world, I adopted managing my outer world to feel seen; and society, along with others around me, reinforced this decision. I dieted to fit the latest ideal. I overspent to appear put together, used drugs and alcohol to be more social, went under the knife in hopes to be desired. I starved, vomited, and held my tongue, all while pushing myself to succeed.

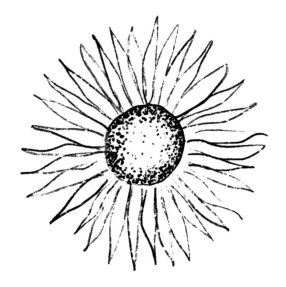

This pattern would become a usual way of life for me. I thought I could sweep away unwanted feelings by shifting focus onto something outside myself. It began with the obsession to "improve" me and slowly seeped into fixing others. To this day, this old pattern shows itself in my thoughts when my body is overwhelmed or stressed. It is through conscious awareness that I choose to witness the thoughts without taking destructive action.

Though I grappled with my experience early on, I always sensed something big was going on within me. While struggling under the weight of it all, I still had an inner pull not to avoid but to follow the pain. But for decades, that sense of higher purpose would lose out to the immensity of my suffering. I could not find the upside to what I was feeling. I did not understand that below the surface of what I believed was a burden was, in fact, some of my unique and most powerful strengths.

"

I did not understand that below
the surface of what I believed
was a burden was, in fact,
some of my unique and
most powerful strengths.

Strengths

Empaths have a sharpened awareness of others' emotions. The magnitude of this experience can often leave them feeling that the negatives of being an empath outweigh the positives. They feel not just their own distress and sorrow but the sadness and fear of others as well. We can be told we are "too sensitive," and without known relief, our heart can feel crushed under the constant weight. Being an empath is not something one can change, but reacquainting ourselves with its benefits and our strengths can lighten the journey and allow us space to better care for ourselves.

STRONG INTUITION

Intuition is the immediate perception of truth, independent of reasoning or understanding. Also called a gut feeling, all humans can home in to their intuitive guidance. If you asked people around you, I bet most will have a story about their gratitude for following their intuition. Empaths not only have the gut feeling intuition but also sense and soak up energy and information into their bodies from others. This ability to feel the subtleties and energy around them is a form of intuition.

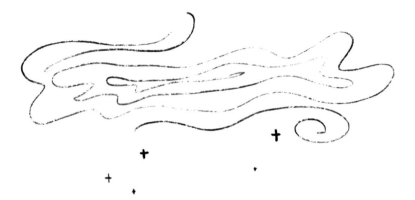

Empaths having a powerful intuition is different from an empath sensing and trusting their intuition. Many empaths share an experience of not feeling safe in their bodies. This stems from the magnitude of what we sense and not having an outlet of relief or escape. Over time, this scary feeling within themselves leads them to disconnect from their bodies.

When we distance ourselves from our bodies, we also detach from our intuitive nudges. How we heal this disconnect from our bodies will be covered in chapter 9. For now, let us familiarize ourselves with the several types of intuition.

Did you know that our intuition functions at various levels and accesses specific senses? How your intuition shows up for you may be different from how my intuition feels to me. In chapter 9, we explore differences in how our intuition manifests in our bodies, including clairvoyance, claircognizance, clairaudience, and clairsentience. An empath's intuition is one of their greatest strengths, and their ability to listen and trust themselves directly impacts their ability to thrive. When they reconnect to their bodies' intelligence and allow their intuition to guide them, they step away from others' energy and see what they need to flourish.

NATURAL HEALER

When an empathetic ear is present, a person begins healing. For many years I carried unhealed trauma. As a highly sensitive child, I picked up every little behavior and energy shift related to people sharing their pain. I noticed that adults did not want to hear about suffering—I saw the shifting of body weight, the blank stares, the rolling of eyes, and the responses meant to shut down and change the topic. I learned that my pain was a burden to others. This was a time in my life when I learned to play down my grief, play up my ability to endure, and pretend I was fine. In short, I learned to hold on to my pain so others could be comfortable. What I did not know was that the act of making others comfortable blocked my ability to process and heal my trauma. Enter coping mechanisms.

Empaths who care for themselves and have healthy boundaries are great listeners, and listening is healing. Research studies reveal that by feeling empathy, your heart rate slows, you release a hormone (oxytocin) that encourages bonding, and the part of your brain that is related to care and pleasure activates. The person being empathetically listened to accesses self-healing through this process, allowing them to let go of frustrations, anxieties, and fear.

Another way the presence of an empath can be healing is the ability to notice the unseen distress of others. This gift can put an empath in a prime spot to offer the healing comfort that someone needs.

HIGHLY CREATIVE

Empaths have a full emotional life—they feel it, and they feel it big. This is a reason empaths and highly sensitive people favor creative ventures, like art, music, writing, or entrepreneurship. These creative outlets allow them to express emotions that others may not understand. Because the emotions and feelings they experience are consistent, they can find themselves turning to their creative ventures with regularity and focus. This steady focus opens them up to turning a creative project into a successful experience.

NOT EASILY MANIPULATED

We already know that empaths notice others' feelings and emotions, but did you know a highly sensitive empath also notices the tiny nuances of behavior, tone of voice, and body language? This trait can make lying to an empath difficult. Multiple studies show that humans, on average, tell untruths twice a day; and when we do lie, some specific clues make it easier to spot.

When someone is untruthful, they are likely to show body cues like fidgeting and specific hand movements. There is also a change in tone of voice and facial signs like complexion changes and eye movements that can point to dishonesty. An empath's ability to notice shifts in energy, feelings, and emotions is a mighty strength; add that to detecting subtle body and behavioral cues that can make an empath an expert lie-spotter. Like every human on this planet, empaths are born with things they are great at and other things they are not. Where they led themselves astray is looking toward others to identify the validity of their gifts.

I have always known I had significant work to do, but the magnitude of what I felt derailed me from my purpose. I believed that strength would not hurt. I thought that anything meant to do good in the world could not be uncomfortable and others would not reject it. I thought everyone wanted to talk about their pain, to move through it. My strengths got lost in a pattern: I would notice the emotion or discrepancy in communication. I would attempt to communicate what I felt. Met with pushback or lashing out, I would retreat and lose trust in myself and others. Over time, the loss of confidence in self and others grew and disconnect from my gifts increased.

I wish I had grasped that my ability to notice emotions and discrepancies was a superpower all along. I wish I had known that people's reactions to what I felt had less to do with the validity of what I perceived and more to do with emotional maturity. But most critical, I wish I understood that an empath's well-being is chiefly dependent on caring for their sensitivities and grasping that the majority of what I perceive is not mine to handle.

EXERCISE: RELEASE SHAME

Grab a piece of paper and something to write with. Beginning with step 1, write as much as you can about each topic. This exercise helps identify and reframe shame; it can also help you see areas where you lack boundaries.

1. List all the areas in which you feel shame.

2. What story is attached to the shame? (For example, "I should be ashamed because _____.")

3. What is the emotional payoff for holding on to the shame (e.g., avoiding change, attention/reassurance from others, staying small or safe)?

4. Where did you learn that shame was necessary to feel?

5. List ways you can get your needs/payoffs met in empowering ways.

6. Do you want to be free from shame? Do you believe you are worthy of being free from shame? Are you willing to let go of shame? Feel into this before you answer.

ch 3 THE EMPATH AND ENERGY

I sum up my early empath experience like this:

Today, life will be different because I will be different. I started each day with pure intentions and high hopes, but when I stepped into the world, my highly sensitive empathic nature kicked in, and my will to thrive turned to a need to survive. As a child, I wanted to enjoy school and the relationships that others enjoyed. I stepped forward with pure love in my heart, but almost immediately, I would be bewildered by what I felt. The incongruences of words versus actions scared me. The ease at which being "cool" surpassed loyalty alarmed me. The way my body felt around others overwhelmed me.

Each morning, decade after decade, the cliché of "you can do it" played in my head. I believed that if I could think positively, smile more prominently, and ignore what I felt, I would influence the energy around me. But at the end of every day, I felt defeated and convinced that escaping the energy I felt was impossible.

I did not understand that my experience was different from others. I did not know that the other girls were not picking up what I was; they did not feel what I felt. At an early age, I began to comprehend that the more I felt, the more uncomfortable I was, and the more uncomfortable I was, the more others pulled back. The more others pulled back, the more my experience validated the belief that something was wrong with me.

Had I understood how to articulate my experience, I might have found the commonality with others I craved. Had I learned as a child that the way I perceived the world was not a mistake, I might have avoided years of emotional trauma. Had I understood human beings' complexity, in that our need to feel loved can equate to denying our feelings, I might not have lost trust in myself and others. Then again, had my experience been different, I would not have taken the path I did, I would not understand what I do now, and I would not be authoring this book for all of you.

"

Everything—including humans and our psychological processes of thought, beliefs, emotions, and consciousness—is composed of unseen-to-the-eye energy.

What Is Energy?

If you have explored the Internet, a school textbook, or a spiritual self-help website, you are familiar with the word *energy*. To know how energy relates to us, we should understand energy in general and scientific terms. Einstein's mathematical equation of $E = mc^2$ provided clarity to scientists all over the world. In his finding, he discovered that energy (E) equals mass (m) times the speed of light (c) squared (2), or $E = mc^2$. The life-changing equation revealed that mass and energy are different forms of the same thing.

According to the First Law of Thermodynamics, the total of the universe's energy is constant, incapable of being created or destroyed. It can only change from one form to another. Energy comes in various forms like solid mass and non-solid matter, heat, light, electrical, sound, gravitational, potential (stored energy), and kinetic (energy of motion). Quantum physics asserts that mass and energy are interchangeable; therefore, mass is simply a manifestation of energy. In short, everything—including humans and our psychological processes of thought, beliefs, emotions, and consciousness—is composed of unseen-to-the-eye energy.

ENERGY FROM AROUND THE WORLD

The mention of feeling energy in spiritual circles could make people uncomfortable if they grew up in the Western region of the world. Often in Western culture, energy is understood as something seen. This definition aligns with Western science. When we confine ourselves to this definition of energy, we limit the broader possibilities and disregard energy's philosophical origins. In the West, we are accustomed to a "see it to believe it" mentality. This view strives to explain the world through a cause precedes effect pattern, meaning all energy has a clear beginning and precise end. There are upsides to discovering exact measurements. We can find how much energy is available to humankind or how it needs to be distributed or allocated. The downside of a cause and effect energy model is that it does not view energy as limitless, nor does it leave space for discovery and imagination.

While the West is more focused on objective science with empirical data and proof, the Eastern philosophies are known for their more wholesome, sensitive, and natural take on energy. For thousands of years, Eastern cultural traditions have honored the belief that energy is beyond what we can see. The Indian-Buddhists believe energy is absolute and that it is indecipherable. In Indian religion and philosophy, the world or maya is an illusion; and the concept of energy is expressed in the word *prana*, meaning "breath or soul." Prana, or life energy, permeates all things, including inanimate objects. Though Western culture focuses more on the presence of something to prove validity and success, Eastern culture believes the unseen, absence of thought, and stillness of mind lift our energy fields, allowing humans to obtain their highest potential.

FEELING ENERGY

What does an empath mean when they say, "This room has heavy energy," or, "I feel low energy around her?" What are they saying about the energy? When an empath says they sense the energy, they are expressing how someone feels to them. An empath is communicating how an environment or the space near another person feels within their body. The empath can determine through premonition (knowing or feeling) many things about an atmosphere, most distinctly the emotional climate. An empath's experience is more than empathy. They do not just recognize others' feelings; they feel the other's physical sensations and emotions in their body.

There is no doubt to the empath that everything is energy and we are all energetic beings. Empaths feel the energetic body that is invisible to the eye. Through bodily experience, the empath knows that an energy exchange goes beyond a casual nod or friendly hug; the empath can sense when things are much more than they appear. Can you remember when you were in a social situation and the energy felt suffocating but you stayed? Can you recall a time when an encounter was draining your energy and you questioned your reality?

Most people are often detached and uninterested in knowing, acknowledging, or feeling anything inside them. As humans, we often fear negative emotions and refuse to visit any uncomfortable circumstance in our life. This pattern can be excruciating to the empath. This avoidance pattern communicates that we must deny and avoid the pain to be happy. The empath who avoids pain and negative emotions ends up detached from themselves and others. What I have found in my life and working with empaths is detachment from self to avoid what we feel is the leading cause of our suffering. Part of embracing the whole of who we are is awareness of our energy and how our body feels in each moment. Specific circumstances will feel draining to you, and there are specific draining experiences for me.

Although deeply affected by the world, empaths are not victims—they control their energy depletion. Many empaths operate from empty energy tanks, so many situations feel tedious. When life feels consistently heavy, and we do not trust ourselves to improve it, we sink into victimhood and blame—and victimhood is a disempowered state of being. When we take full accountability for our energy and stay conscious of our body, thoughts, and feelings, we can see the steps to care for ourselves.

SPOTTING ENERGY DRAINS

How do empaths spot an energy drain? It begins by connecting back to their bodies and noticing how they feel in each moment. The better they get at the mind-body connection, the better they will recognize their energy drains and act before they burn out. Common signs of energy drains for empaths can be finding it extremely difficult to be present. Empaths depend on distractions like their phones or focusing on others' problems to get them through the day.

Another sign is that they feel a heavy emotion like fear, sorrow, or anxiety and do not know why. When they do not understand where their feelings come from, it can be that they were not noticing their thoughts, or it can be a sign of depleted energy. Sleep patterns can alert them to energy drains. If they are getting adequate sleep and their health is optimal but they still feel depleted upon waking, it might be necessary to look more closely at our environment. An ever-changing mood or shortness with others can also be signs that there's a lack in life force energy. Once they notice how their body feels in each moment, they will discern what circumstances drain them the most.

COMMON ENERGY DRAINS

Though empaths cannot turn off their sensitivities, they can become aware of their limits. When they take accountability for their energy drains and make the changes required to thrive, they call back their power and leave victimhood behind.

Lack of Sleep

Sleep is necessary for human survival. After as little as three days, our body and mind deteriorate. Empaths need a consistent sleep pattern to feel their best. Empaths are highly sensitive in all aspects of our lives, including their body's response to not receiving enough rest. Deep sleep is essential to lessen the overstimulation they experience each day of their lives.

I require no less than eight hours of sleep each night, and my bedtime needs to be before midnight. If I do not grant myself the rest I need, I experience things like nausea, depressed mood, mind fog, and anxiety. For years I resisted giving my body what it needed for fear of missing out or to circumvent looks I would get from others when leaving a party early.

Because they are hypersensitive to stimuli, empaths may struggle to calm their mind before bed. This issue can cause the empath to lose much-needed rest. Creating a calming bedtime routine, including meditation and turning technology off two hours before bed, can help calm the mind. Empaths are also prone to stress-related illness such as adrenal fatigue, an imbalance in the endocrine system that can also play a part in sleep disruption. Giving your body the support it needs, whether through supplements, naturopaths, or doctors, ensures your body will calm when it is time for rest.

Lack of Alone Time

Empaths are super responsive to the energy around others. They are like antennas noticing every little signal that others miss. Empaths are highly sensitive people, which means they have reactive nervous systems. With a reactive nervous system, the outer world easily inundates them. Harmony is challenging to obtain when surrounded by other people, noises, and various stimuli. So, empaths need regular alone time and moments of pause throughout the day to refocus and restore. The solitude an empath needs is not about avoidance and unhealthy isolation; it is about self-preservation and self-care.

Violent Content

Do you have a friend that loves horror movies or one that will not miss the next episode of their favorite true crime series? Although not all empaths are affected equally, violent content can be agony for some. You know that suspenseful feeling you get when the teens are running from the killer in the woods? To some, it is a welcomed rush of adrenaline; to empaths, fake and real-life violence can leave our nervous system fired up for hours or even days, making watching violent content a threat to our well-being. Understanding that violence can adversely affect us is one thing, but taking the necessary steps to limit it is another. We live in a society that glorifies violence in movies, news, and television. Many people are accustomed to seeing it and may scoff at your decision to distance from it. Remember, you are not like them, you do not need to be like them, and your well-being is your responsibility.

Loud Noise

Loud noise, smells, and excessive talking can easily fray an empath's nerves. Like being sensitive to others' emotions, empaths can have a low threshold for the stimulation of light, sound, and smell. Because of these, they favor more low-key settings, such as coffee shops or friends' houses, over noisy clubs or parties. The next time you are in a loud environment, pay attention to your body, your feel for cues, and your body response to the noise. When does your body begin to feel affected? What physical clues does your body present when it needs a recess from its surroundings?

A few ways this sensitivity shows up for me is my need to turn the radio down if I am driving in an unfamiliar area or my need to have background noise at a minimum if I am having a deep conversation. Background noise does not affect others as much as it does me. I need the stimulus to be minimal for me to give full focus.

Excessive Negativity

There is no denying it—stress exists. All of us have experienced it and have caused it for others. The human journey is one of balance between shadow (pain, stress, sorrow) and light (joy, gratitude, positivity). To deny the shadow is to deny the whole of who we are. To grow into our full power, we must embrace our imperfections. Although the balance between our darkness and light is essential for self-acceptance, some seem to prioritize living under a dark cloud and sharing their unpleasantness. These people consistently talk malevolently of people, places, and pastimes, draining the joy out of life.

Science acknowledges that spending excessive time around those continually complaining or discontented with the world harms our health and happiness. Studies show that prolonged stress modifies gene expression in our immune system. Our genes being modified means we become sick by hanging out with angry, discouraging, or demoralizing people too long. Empaths can be affected quickly and more deeply by the negativity around them, and it can take their systems longer to recover. When they encounter people struggling, there are a couple of things to assess.

First, is this person moving through a temporary difficult stage of life and grappling with sorting it out, or has this person been in a constant state of torment for the majority of their life? Second, how does my body feel around this person? How much time am I able to spend with this person before my well-being is affected? What boundaries do I need to maintain my peace? And compassion? Empaths are natural listeners and typically want to ease others' pain, but we cannot help others to our detriment. We cannot help others out of the dark by leading ourselves into the darkness.

Crowded Place

Empaths can become overwhelmed in large or small groups. Being around many people can magnify our empathy. For years I thought I had social anxiety. When in large groups or crowds, I would feel uneasy and anxious. Believing something was wrong with me, I would look for an escape. I would turn to a few glasses of wine or attach to one person who felt safe and bide my time miserably. Pretending I did not feel the angst, fear, and heaviness around me had a tremendous impact on my mental and physical health.

"

To deny the shadow is to deny
the whole of who we are.

Many empaths have similar experiences. They compare their social experiences to others and believe they, as empaths, should manage them better. Assuming they are flawed, they find distractions to get through, hoping the next time will be better. The longer one denies self-acceptance and soothing support, the more likely it is to develop stress-related illnesses. Symptoms like excessive resentment, social anxiety, and adrenal fatigue can appear. Empaths become fearful of what their body feels like around others and believe they have no control over their experience.

Small Talk

Small talk is a pleasant conversation that does not go deep or touch on controversial topics. Small talk focuses on a surface topic. We usually stick to small talk when we meet people for the first time or when we are not vested in building connections with others. You might use it on an airplane with someone sitting next to you or with a neighbor you pass on your daily walk. Small talk can be asking about the weather or asking if someone is looking forward to the weekend. Small talk is mostly observation; it does not contain a profound substance. Small talk is a natural occurrence when building trust and connection with a new acquaintance.

Empaths are deep people (they sense the big stuff). This can make small talk uncomfortable for them. They want to talk about the real stuff that affects the people in our world. They want to talk about the things they already sense and feel. Small talk to empaths is a superficial conversation that bypasses the real topics that would make a real difference. It is challenging for them to feel grief from another and still talk about the day of the week. It feels inauthentic and awkward to talk about the weather when the empath senses the more pressing issues and conversations under the surface subject.

Learning to balance small talk with deep dives is essential for empaths. Thriving socially means understanding we all have unique needs, and avoiding all small talk can be isolating. Some people may not want to deep dive into conversations, and that is okay. But the empath needs to find others who, like them, enjoy going beyond the surface.

Feeling Rushed

Most empaths are highly sensitive, meaning they have a sensory processing sensitivity. When they notice stimuli, they process each one with great depth. Because they process things more deeply, they require more time to reconcile and recover. Depth of processing plays a part in an empath's need to plan and think and respond to everything. They naturally and intensely analyze information or responsibilities in their daily lives, and being rushed hinders their more profound, often gradual rate of processing. Feeling rushed bypasses an empath's natural flow, and this can make them anxious and stressed. The need for natural flow is why having a packed schedule, hopping from one responsibility to the next without any time to process, leaves me anxious, emotional, and resentful. I thought women naturally excelled at multitasking. I did not understand why I could not simultaneously brush my teeth and pick out my clothes without feeling anxiety throughout my body.

Committing to writing this book created anxiety until I outlined how to manage a slower, more intentional writing schedule. I recognized that a couple of hours of writing each day would yield me the downtime and space needed to handle my other responsibilities while delivering to the publisher on time. Empaths are great decision makers. They take the time and think through all aspects of each choice. When they decide quickly, their intuition makes the option super clear, and they trust their gut implicitly.

Conflicts and Arguments

Can you recall the last intense argument you had with a partner or a coworker? How did the anger show up in your body? Was the anger a tightness in your throat, or did it feel like energy wanting to escape from your chest? For empaths, everything they feel and experience during a conflict is compounded. They not only profoundly feel their feelings, but they also feel the other person's torment. Because everyone's feelings are intense in an argument, fights significantly affect empaths.

Empaths cannot merely exchange apologies, take a deep breath, and walk away feeling aligned. They require adequate time to sort and release all the feelings that swirl in their bodies. They need rest to restore their nervous system after being overstimulated. They need to give themselves the grace required to see the resentment they feel toward others who do not seem similarly affected by the experience. For many years, I allowed resentment to grow toward my husband. When he needs to express frustration in a conversation or at a football game, he swiftly and intensely shows it. After putting his heavy feelings out there, he can go about his business as if nothing happened. I do not have the same luxury. When my husband expresses anger toward anything, and I am close by, it feels like a punch in the gut. My heart rate quickens, my chest tightens, and my throat closes. The football game goes to a commercial, and my husband appears unfazed. However, my nervous system is in fight-or-flight mode. For years, I resisted disruption to my peace and felt powerless to change my experience. I held resentment toward anyone and any emotions that caused dysregulation to my nervous system.

After years of striving to no avail to soothe, manage, and change how he expressed frustration, I grew incredibly resentful of him. I did not understand why what he felt affected me so profoundly, so it was impossible to communicate to him what I needed effectively. To him, it felt a lot like criticism and control—and to an extent, it was. I saw his feelings as a threat to my harmony, and for me to feel better, he needed to change. As I began to understand myself as a highly sensitive empath, I could communicate my needs more clearly. I began setting necessary boundaries and giving myself the space I needed. Genuinely understanding myself created space for my husband to explore alternatives when expressing frustration, ways that feel less threatening within my body.

An empath's ability to live life to the fullest is connected to self-awareness. They must know what works for them and what does not. They need to know what circumstances drain them and make them feel alive with energy. Most importantly, they must act based on self-awareness. Knowing they are empaths is not enough.

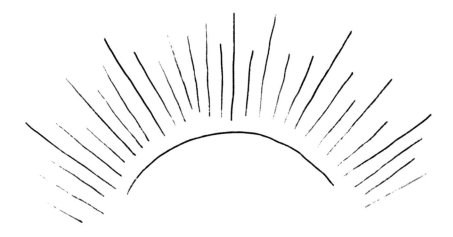

To create the life we want, a life where we feel everything immensely but not to our detriment, we have to make life changes. So, what stops us from making the necessary changes in our lives?

I had to sort through all kinds of feelings, emotions, and beliefs that kept me from change. I went through feelings of guilt ("Who am I to do this?"), I experienced fear ("They will not stick around."), and I felt dread ("What if this does not work?"). I discovered that it was my unhealed trauma holding me apart from the life I desired. To have the type of life experience I wanted, I had to make healing a priority. Think about it: If we feel and process everything to the maximum, we are affected by our traumatic experiences this way, too. The pain we avoid can be why we are not able to step into a more fulfilling life.

ch 4 THE EMPATH AND TRAUMA

When you hear descriptive
details about someone like they
are highly empathic,

have keen senses, notice subtleties, and tune into others'
mood shifts, do you think, "They're an empath?" They may
be an empath, but did you know these descriptive details
also describe a trauma survivor? Hypervigilance is a state
of heightened alertness. In a state of hypervigilance, you
are extremely sensitive to subtleties in your surroundings.
Hypervigilance can be the brain's way of adapting to trauma.
To minimize the reoccurrence of the trauma, the subconscious mind continually scans the environment to anticipate
danger. As a result, our senses are on high alert, ready to
spot and respond to any risk.

Some researchers believe that 50 to 70 percent of humans have experienced trauma; it is closer to 100 percent. A traumatizing event can be any situation someone has difficulty coping with and finds physically or emotionally threatening. Some events would traumatize any of us, and some, because of differences in temperament and sensitivity, may traumatize you but not others. We already know empaths are extremely sensitive to things occurring around them and process things longer and more intensely than others. This sensitivity means that a situation that is temporarily stressful for one could be traumatizing to you. How something uniquely affects you does not mean something is amiss or better about them for overcoming sooner. It means our brains and nervous systems process differently, and we require individual attention and care.

There are three types of trauma: acute, resulting from a single stressful or dangerous event; chronic; rising from repeated and continued exposure to highly stressful events; and complex, emerging from exposure to multiple traumatic events. Throughout my childhood, I was bullied—not mildly teased but consistently and habitually singled out, tormented, and publicly shunned. Bullying is considered chronic trauma in its repeated and continued exposure. The bullying lasted throughout my school years and had a profound impact on my health. Each morning I would wake knowing what was coming. I had no control over others' behavior, and school seemed nonnegotiable. I felt powerless over my circumstances. I grew up when childhood bullying was common and overlooked and science did not understand the long-term effects. Statements like "They must like you if they tease you" were typical and highly inaccurate.

Why Is It Helpful for Us to Acknowledge Our Trauma?

First and foremost, we all deserve self-compassion, peace, and healing.

Second, when we know what behaviors and thoughts come from trauma, we can distinguish our negative thoughts and feelings from others' thoughts and feelings. For example, I am in a social situation, and the words of another hurt someone near me. If I am not aware of my trauma and how certain circumstances trigger past pain, I will think the torment I feel is about how the other person feels. This is called projection. When we are unaware of how our trauma presents itself within us, we may confuse what we feel for others' pain or energy.

Our empathy is real. Our ability to feel into other people's experiences is legitimate, but how we filter that through our minds until we are aware of our trauma is most likely a projection.

"

If I am not aware of my trauma and how certain circumstances trigger past pain, I will think the torment I feel is about how the other person feels.

The Brain and Trauma

For decades, the word *trauma* described events like soldiers returning from war, rape, and severe abuse. These events would be traumatizing for all of us. But through the years, I have noticed that matching "trauma" to only extreme examples leads people who have not had a labeled "extreme event" to slip through the cracks of care. The old saying "it could be worse" can lead us to deny ourselves the support we need to overcome the things that hurt us.

The American Psychological Association defines *trauma* as "1. any disturbing experience that results in significant fear, helplessness, dissociation, confusion, or other disruptive feelings intense enough to have a long-lasting negative effect on a person's attitudes, behavior, and other aspects of functioning. Traumatic events include those caused by human behavior (e.g., rape, war, industrial accidents) as well as by nature (e.g., earthquakes) and often challenge an individual's view of the world as a just, safe, and predictable place. 2. any serious physical injury, such as a widespread burn or a blow to the head." Although responses to trauma can vary, trauma can change our brain in some foreseen ways. Understanding these changes to our brain can help us recognize our specific needs and assist with our self-compassion levels. We understand how our brain is processing the world. We can seek support and learn skills to rewire our brain for healing.

Brain Changes After Trauma

Trauma can change brain functioning in several ways, but three of the most significant changes occur in the prefrontal cortex, the anterior cingulate cortex, and the amygdala. The prefrontal cortex (PFC), or "thinking center," is behind your forehead at the top of your brain. The PFC allows us clarity of thought, allows us to make sound decisions, and brings awareness to ourselves and others. After trauma or when our trauma is triggered (aroused), the PFC lags, slowing and altering the benefits of the thinking center.

The anterior cingulate cortex (ACC), or "emotion regulation center," is near the PFC and works closely with the thinking center. The ACC has a leading role in regulating emotions. When the ACC is in healthy working order, we can manage complex thoughts and feelings without being overwhelmed. Sure, we may have the urge to tell off our rude boss, but our emotion regulation center steers us from doing something we would regret.

Our amygdala, or "fear center," is deep within our brain; and its function is outside our conscious control. The amygdala's responsibility is to receive everything we see, hear, touch, smell, and taste and answer one question: "Is this safe?" The fear center detects danger and threats and creates fear within us to act. When afflicted by trauma, our amygdala can be overactive, leaving us to feel more afraid, reactive, and hypervigilant.

Empath or Trauma Survivor?

Many have reached out to me wanting to know if they are an empath, a trauma survivor, or both. My answer is always the same: No one can answer that question for you. The answer lies within you, but the joy you experience in your life is dependent on understanding yourself and prioritizing your healing. Empaths and highly sensitive people are like everyone in that they can all be traumatized by similar things. What makes them different is that they feel everything to its extreme, and sometimes they notice distress that others are not aware of.

If a child or an adult does not know they are highly sensitive or does not understand how to care for their unique needs, their day-to-day experience can be traumatizing. An empath overwhelmed by daily life can develop a fear of others, a disconnect from their body, and disdain for who they are. In short, they do not feel safe being themselves.

An empath, continually afraid of what they may feel when they leave the house, may develop acute stress. When under continual stress, our sympathetic nervous system steps in to help. When our mind communicates a threat, the sympathetic nervous system stimulates the adrenal glands, triggering catecholamines' release (including adrenaline and noradrenaline). Catecholamines help the body respond to stress and prepare the body for fight-or-flight reactions. The phrase *fight or flight* describes the body's urge to fight or run for survival.

Centuries ago, the fight-or-flight response would have helped us stave off a saber-toothed tiger. This biological response of the sympathetic nervous system is one of the most powerful we have as humans. The hypothetical cave person encountered the saber-toothed tiger a few times in a lifetime. The power of the sympathetic nervous system kicked in, and the cave person survived without much issue. Today's saber-toothed tiger is inner trauma and emotional stress. The empath who does not understand how to minimize what they feel can be in constant fear and anxiety, and their body responds as if that tiger is chasing them.

When we spend most of our time fighting or fleeing, our adrenal glands begin to weaken, making it even more difficult for us to handle the smallest stressor. You can see the merry-go-round effect here, right? I have been nursing my adrenal glands back to health for three years. It is a very delicate process, including consistent awareness of my body, environment, and commitment to a lifestyle that caters to my sensitive needs.

In Dr. Elaine Aron's research, she concludes that highly sensitive people make up 2 to 3 percent of the population. That means that close to 98 percent of the population does not experience the world as I do. Being highly unique increases the chances of rejection and being disregarded for how I interpret the world. Empaths' abilities can come with a lifetime of societal invalidation. Most of them learn that their feelings and abilities are not welcome at an early age, especially if others benefit from shielding themselves and others from the truth or things that do not "feel good." Dismissal and shunning of our feelings can create self-doubt that leaves us withholding our feelings, denying ourselves the support we deserve, and ultimately believing there is something innately wrong with us—all of which lead to prolonged stress and suffering.

"

An empath overwhelmed by daily life can develop a fear of others, a disconnect from their body, and disdain for who they are. In short, they do not feel safe being themselves.

COMMON TRAUMA SYMPTOMS

Shame

Shame is a very destructive emotion that many of us can face in our life. Shame is different from other emotions because it exists overwhelmingly without any real purpose, unlike guilt. Shame harms us psychologically by blaming us for the things that cause us pain and condemning us for others' hurtful actions. Shame causes harm to someone's self-image as no other emotion can. Shame can make us feel deeply flawed, worthless, and unlovable. Shame is the act of judging ourselves. Guilt says, "I wish I had not done that; it was not kind. I will do better next time." Shame says, "I am a horrible person for doing that." Guilt creates space for change; shame permanently condemns. Many empaths and highly sensitive people are told they are too much or too sensitive. This can lead to shame and a desire to be something other than they are.

If someone experiences enough shame, they can become self-loathing to the point that they become self-destructive or suicidal. Shame is responsible for a wide array of problems. Shame-induced behaviors include self-criticism, self-blame, self-neglect, self-destruction, self-sabotage, perfectionism, and most importantly, staying in cycles of abuse. By enhancing self-compassion, we can offset shame and create a new, more positive perception of ourselves. When we start to accept ourselves for precisely who we are, apart from what others think, we can diminish the intensity of shame.

Avoidance

Avoidance usually corresponds with anxiety (excessive worry or uneasiness). After years of overwhelm or not understanding why they experience life as they do, empaths may begin to avoid people, places, or circumstances, hoping to lighten unpleasant feelings and emotions. Initially, avoidance feels like a relief; but over time, anxiety grows and the belief that we cannot handle our feelings strengthens, leading to a substantial need to avoid. Avoidance can be necessary to tend to our emotional needs. This isolation can be healthy and essential for self-care and comes from self-awareness and consciousness.

Extreme Alertness

Some empaths are afraid of their day-to-day life. Believing they are powerless over what they feel and perceive, some can worry about what they will sense around others. A constant state of fear can lead to a hypervigilant state (continually scanning our environment for threats). A hypervigilant state is a nervous system pushed to its limit. Hypervigilance is a state of enhanced alertness. If you are in a state of hypervigilance, you are extremely sensitive to your environment. Hypervigilance can make you feel like you are observant of unseen dangers, whether from people or your environment. Many times, in a hypervigilant state, the threats we perceive are not real. When our nervous system reacts to a social event as a threat, our body sends feedback to our mind, and our mind produces thoughts that reinforce our fear.

These disempowering thoughts, usually rooted in self-doubt, can become repet-itive and replay when we are afraid—thoughts like "No one likes me," or "I am being judged," or any false belief of unworthiness. Our reaction to a new social experience is rooted in our past, and hypervigilance was created to keep us safe in an early encounter. Empaths who develop hypervigilance may confuse it for noticing someone else's negative energy. When one confuses a trauma response to someone's energy, it creates more self-doubt and fear, which causes unneeded struggle in relationships. The increased fear reinforces and strengthens a hyper-vigilant state, and eventually we believe empaths are destined to suffer.

Feeling Different

A belief that typically accompanies trauma is that empaths are different from others. The difference I refer to is not "I have this amazing uniqueness that makes me differ-ent" but a shame-evoking belief that they are fundamentally broken and continually misunderstood. An empath, repetitively rejected for who they are or for how they feel, may develop shame. Shame frequently accompanies a feeling of alienation and the belief of being "broken beyond repair." The empath and the highly sensitive person cannot turn off how they experience the world. They can develop resilience and prioritize self-care, which helps them bounce back after emotional encounters; but they cannot turn off how the world affects them or change the depth of what they experience.

Empaths may believe that others will never fully understand their experience. They may think that sharing their feelings and thoughts related to their experience will fall on unwelcome ears. Many of them as children noticed they were not like the majority. Many empaths, including myself, spend years trying to crack the code of walking through life, not noticing or feeling so much, and perfecting the art of pretending everything is fine.

One of the most self-healing things I did was to begin writing. I started by writing short articles and submitted them to different publications. I wrote because I felt misunderstood and belittled for my truth. I published them because I was tired of speaking words only to have them argued with, pushed aside, or ignored. I wrote because I knew my words were worth hearing, and I realized I was expressing myself to the wrong people. When the replies and emails began flooding in, I knew I had found my people. I have proof that other humans experience life as I do, and the words I wrote were as healing to them as their replies were to me.

Codependency

A possible outcome of lived trauma is codependent relationships and a likelihood that new connections will struggle. Many descriptions of codependency exist in research. Most studies recognize that it is a learned behavior stemming from dysfunctional families. Codependency manifests from the neglect of personal needs. It usually includes the expectation to focus on someone else's needs and feelings, as well as a dependency on others for emotional support and approval.

Codependency is damaging, and it is common. A codependent relationship is harmful and unilateral, with one person relying on the other to meet most of their needs. There are two roles in a codependent relationship: the fixer, who learned needs are met when they tend to others, and the seeker, who seeks out others to meet their needs. Each person in a codependent relationship will encourage the other, enabling the toxic pattern to continue. Relationships and people are unique, but people entangled in codependent relationships have everyday struggles such as the following:

- *Low self-esteem:* Instead of meeting your own needs and expanding self-esteem, codependents focus on meeting the needs of others. Instead of figuring out how we feel, we are entangled in others' feelings. As children, the responsibility for another's happiness is placed on us.

- *Lack of boundaries:* The source of most conflict and strife within ourselves and our relationships is a lack of boundaries. The codependent is prepared to compromise their needs and happiness to build a relationship with a person who will never be fulfilled.

- **A need to please and take care of others:** The inequity in codependent relationships is apparent, but fear of rejection and confrontation keep the codependent person from change.

- **High sensitivity:** Overly sensitive children can tune in to their parents' emotions and needs. This can create a codependent family dynamic early on in life. The toll of dysfunctional relationships makes us more likely to overreact emotionally to situations.

- **Poor communication:** Due to overfocusing on others' needs, empaths often become unaware of their own wants and needs. It is also common to be reluctant in expressing their needs for fear of being seen as a burden or denied.

It is not unusual for an empath to have codependent tendencies, especially if they grew up in a household that lacked boundaries and with adults who modeled codependent behavior. Young empaths and highly sensitive children notice others' emotions and feelings. They learn that certain emotions expressed by adults make their lives more challenging. To minimize how others' energy feels, they may develop behaviors and tendencies to soothe and "fix" others, to their detriment.

Difficulty Regulating Emotions

Empaths can find it difficult to regulate or manage their emotions. Regulating emotions is the ability to exert restraint over one's emotional status. It may involve rethinking a challenging situation to diminish anger or reframing a thought to lessen anxiety or focusing on reasons to be grateful or calm. Difficulty regulating emotions is common in people with unhealed trauma. Adults whose parents modeled anger as a first and only response will have trouble with emotional regulations, and an empath who feels overwhelmed by others can struggle to regulate. In both scenarios, emotions such as anger, anxiety, sadness, and shame can feel impossible to manage.

Strong feelings like anger can help prepare our bodies to fight when we are genuinely threatened. Big emotions can also help us get things done or to stand up for our needs. Big emotions can also create a toxic, stressful, and traumatic environment for others, especially highly sensitive people. Unhealed trauma will traumatize others. Often when we feel incapable of managing our feelings, we turn to unhealthy distractions or substances, hoping to regain emotional stability. For instance, it is common for an empath to focus on someone else's problems and attempt to fix them to distract from their own healing. How they use their emotions boils down to how the adults in their lives modeled expressing their feelings and the effect of trauma in their lives. Both scenarios require taking accountability for themselves, getting the help they need, and relearning a healthier way to communicate. We must break the cycle.

66

As empaths, their nervous systems are more vividly aware; therefore, they have an increased liklihood of being adversely affected by all stimuli.

Difficulty Maintaining Close Relationships

When humans are hurt, it is natural and biological to do what we can to prevent more hurt. Remember, after trauma, our nervous systems become hypervigilant in hopes of seeking out potential danger. When our body is in a state of assessing risk, we can feel like we did during the original trauma. The chest tightens, our breath quickens, we are overtaken by fear, our thoughts become intrusive and disempowering—and they validate our fear.

Survival is in our DNA. Our fight-or-flight response is a survival mechanism, enabling us to react swiftly to life-threatening conditions. When we are deeply harmed emotionally or physically by another human, our mind and body can register all humans as a potential threat. Living through traumatic experiences can cause us to anticipate danger, disloyalty, or possible harm with new or current relationships. Those who have survived trauma may feel vulnerable and uncertain about what is safe, and it can be tough to trust others, even those we trusted before.

Trauma can cause us to fear getting close to people or believe the world is an unsafe place. Overcome by worry, some may become aggressive or attempt to control others' behavior, hoping to bring about a false sense of safety or predictability. Behaviors like hypervigilance and control can be troubling to those affected and warrant boundaries, but they are natural reactions to a person who feels threatened.

THE PROBABILITY OF TRAUMA

Are empaths and highly sensitive people more likely to experience trauma? They are. As empaths, their nervous systems are more vividly aware; therefore, they have an increased likelihood of being adversely affected by all stimuli. Any negative experiences they have and the emotions that follow they feel to the highest degree. If they grew up in an unsupportive environment overwhelmed by their feelings and emotions, they are more likely to be adversely affected. In contrast, surrounded by those who understand their temperament and needs, they are more likely to flourish.

It is essential for an empath's well-being to not compare or judge what affects them versus what did not affect another. What was traumatic for you? Was anything too profound for your nervous system to process? Only we can say what was traumatic for us. Our experiences combined with our genetics and nervous system make what deeply affects us a very personal thing. You are not alone if your trauma makes your life complicated. If you find that your past experiences create recurring pain for you, you are not alone.

Here are some suggestions and healing modalities I turned to on my journey of healing.

- Self-compassion is essential in healing our deep-seated pain. Healing is challenging work, and showing ourselves love will get us through the days we want to give up.

- Therapists can be another great asset in your healing. A counselor trained in EMDR (eye movement desensitization and reprocessing) made an impact in healing my trauma.

- Establishing a daily meditation practice is essential to create space for peace of mind. Many empaths feel disconnected from their bodies, and meditation allows time to tune in to body sensations.

- Moving our bodies helps move our energy, and intentional movement allows us to return to our bodies.

- When we are healing, it is essential to have supportive relationships. The relationship with ourselves counts, too. We should surround ourselves with others who offer kindness, acceptance, and patience as we wade through deep waters.

Healing trauma can be a lot to take in, but the benefits to an empath are infinite. When they heal their trauma, they restore their nervous system. When they restore their nervous system, they heal the emotions stored in their bodies. When they heal the emotions in their bodies, they free their empathic gifts. When they release their empathic skills, they raise their energy field. When they raise their energetic field, their reality changes.

Identifying Trauma

If you are curious about the trauma you have endured and wonder how those experiences affect you today, your ACEs (adverse childhood experiences) score is a wonderful place to begin.

ACEs represent adverse childhood experiences that harm a child's developing brain and change how we respond to stress. Our brain's changes cause a weakening of our immune systems that affect us for years, even decades in the future. As stated in the CDC-Kaiser Adverse Childhood Experiences Study, ACEs cause most of the chronic disease and mental illness and are at the center of most violence. The ACE Study has published nearly 70 research papers since 1998, and hundreds of supplementary research papers that reference the ACE Study have been published.

Below you will find the basic ACE quiz as referenced in the CDC-Kaiser study and included on www.acestoohigh.com. Please note that there are childhood traumas not included in this basic quiz but that count as ACEs, including bullying, racism, witnessing abuse, death of loved ones, substance abuse by loved ones, and much more. This quiz includes the top ten traumas that the study participants reported.

I highly recommend visiting www.acestoohigh.com and reading as much as you can about this study and the data collected.

BEFORE YOUR 18TH BIRTHDAY:

1. Did a parent or other adult in the household often or very often . . . Swear at you, insult you, put you down, or humiliate you? Or act in a way that made you afraid that you might be physically hurt?

   No ___ If Yes, enter 1 ___

2. Did a parent or other adult in the household often or very often . . . Push, grab, slap, or throw something at you? Or ever hit you so hard that you had marks or were injured?

   No ___ If Yes, enter 1 ___

3. Did an adult or person at least five years older than you ever . . . Touch or fondle you, or have you sexually touch their body? Or attempt or have oral, anal, or vaginal intercourse with you?

   No ___ If Yes, enter 1 ___

4. Did you often or very often feel that . . . No one in your family loved you or thought you were important or special? Or your family did not look out for each other, feel close to each other, or support each other?

No ___ If Yes, enter 1 ___

5. Did you often or very often feel that . . . You didn't have enough to eat, had to wear dirty clothes, and had no one to protect you? Or your parents were too drunk or high to take care of you or take you to the doctor if you needed it?

No ___ If Yes, enter 1 ___

6. Were your parents ever separated or divorced?

No ___ If Yes, enter 1 ___

7. Was your mother or stepmother: Often or very often pushed, grabbed, slapped, or had something thrown at her? Or sometimes, often, or very often kicked, bitten, hit with a fist, or hit with something hard? Or ever repeatedly hit over at least a few minutes or threatened with a gun or knife?

No ___ If Yes, enter 1 ___

8. Did you live with anyone who was a problem drinker or alcoholic, or who used street drugs?

No ___ If Yes, enter 1 ___

9. Was a household member depressed or mentally ill, or did a household member attempt suicide?

No ___ If Yes, enter 1 ___

10. Did a household member go to prison?

No ___ If Yes, enter 1 ___

Now add up your "Yes" answers: ___ This is your ACE Score.

Please visit www.acestoohigh.com to learn more about your score.

Part II

THE HEALED EMPATH

The healed empath is an empath who embraces their unique traits, understands and accepts their sensitivity, and is willing to embrace a lifestyle that caters to their needs. Healed is not a destination of good vibes only or arriving at a place where pain does not exist. That place is not attainable. "Healed," as referred to in this book, implies the awareness of our pain, feelings, thoughts, trauma, energy, how it all shows up in our body, and the action we take to care for ourselves. Healed in this book's context signifies we are willing to experience it all and take accountability for our needs on a moment-to-moment basis and create the life we need to thrive.

A healed empath knows that all humans are light and shadow, strength and weakness; and it is only when they embrace the whole of who they are that they can live in peace with themselves. A healed empath is willing to navigate the darker side of themselves and understands that diving into the shadow can bring them more light. A healed empath understands that healing is not the absence of pain but the awareness of their power and resilience to walk through it.

Empaths can live among heavy energy and thrive. They do this by creating a lifestyle that focuses on self-awareness, building mental resilience, creating boundaries, nurturing their energy, and connecting to their intuition. When empaths incorporate these areas of focus into their lives, they accept the responsibility for their well-being and move fully into their power.

ch 5 SELF-AWARENESS

Self-awareness is essential for empaths;

it is their ability to understand themselves and have an in-depth insight into what makes them who they are. When we are self-aware, we know our strengths and weaknesses and what triggers our emotions and reactions. As we change and grow, our self-awareness allows us to meet our evolving needs.

As my self-awareness grew, I became conscious of how my thoughts changed and my body felt during the third week of my menstrual cycle. Like clockwork, on the third week of my cycle, my body begins to feel heavy and my thoughts become self-judgmental. For years, I took to the mind and body shift like a moth to a flame, and I would respond in similar ways. For decades, I assaulted myself with the same thoughts at the same time each month, driving me to spend thousands of dollars on diet crazes and body-shrinking gimmicks. The pattern's consistency was mind-blowing. What was most astonishing was my unawareness of its repetitive nature and how my cycle unconsciously pulled me into darkness every month.

The shift still occurs every month, but what has changed is my reaction to it. Now when I stand in my closet, I notice my thoughts rejecting my body in every outfit. I observe the judgment and the tension in my body and at once check the calendar. I remind myself that what is happening is a deep pattern rooted in a painful childhood experience. I take a deep breath and redirect my mind to soothing affirming thoughts. The pattern is there, but my reaction is changing. I release myself from torment and self-sabotage.

Self-awareness is useful in reaching greater fulfillment in life. When we are self-aware, we have more gratifying relationships and better communication. We make sounder decisions and manage our emotions more efficiently. When we are self-aware, we notice what comes up for us in real time so we can take the steps needed to care for ourselves and others. An empath who is self-aware is more likely to notice when their body is feeling stress and when their thoughts have taken a dark turn. A self-aware empath can more easily intercede before they crash and burn. Knowing ourselves allows us to course-correct when needed and make or cancel plans to benefit our well-being. A self-aware empath can differentiate their energy from another. When a self-aware empath notices outside energy, they will understand how to best care for themselves and set healthy boundaries. Although self-awareness is beneficial to our well-being in many ways, some studies suggest that only 10 to 15 percent of people are self-aware.

What Holds Us Apart from Self-Awareness?

Self-awareness can be difficult for us. Whoever produced the saying "the truth hurts" was not kidding. We are all working on self-acceptance, and sometimes when self-love is lacking, we can be closed off to constructive feedback.

Self-awareness can be painful for others. Did you know that the more successful someone is, the less likely they are to be self-aware? The odds of a successful person being self-aware decrease due to a lack of honest feedback. It is important to note that I may define *success* differently than you; therefore, this effect can happen in various situations. Successful people are less likely to get constructive criticism because people fear repercussions.

We may have a misguided goal of "good vibes only." It may be surprising to hear, but the bulk of the self-help movement has undermined self-awareness. Instead, self-esteem rather than self-awareness is celebrated, recommending that people ignore negative thoughts and disregard outside feedback. The focus on self-esteem has created a feel-good-only standard. This standard enables narcissistic tendencies, making it difficult for people to embrace input that does not feel good.

SIGNS WE MAY LACK SELF-AWARENESS

One sign of low self-awareness is repetitive negative patterns of thought and behavior. I showed a recurring emotional pattern in the example on page 83. I shared that it occurred every month for decades without question. The negative emotional pattern repeated because I was not stepping outside of my experience to witness it happening. The higher our self-awareness, the more likely we see our negative emotional patterns. Recognize what creates the pattern and take steps to heal.

Another sign that we lack self-awareness is our habit of choosing distractions and calling them self-care. Here is an example: I have had a grueling day. I feel tired and a tad anxious, and my patience is gone. I sit on the couch and pick up my phone. I spend the next two hours scrolling through Instagram. Scrolling Instagram is not the issue; the problem is that I tell myself it is self-care. I need a break from my day. If I pay attention, though, I notice that my anxiety has gotten worse and my patience has taken a hit. Lack of self-awareness will have us calling distractions self-care and doing things that do not make us feel better.

How Self-Aware Are You?

From one to ten, how self-aware are you? Do you think you're above average in your level of self-awareness? I will be the first to say that I have prided myself on my elevated level of self-awareness.

A 2016 research study out of Yale University discovered that almost 80 percent of people believe they are in the top 50 percent on standard emotional intelligence tests. Psychologists call our tendency to think we are more proficient than we are the "superiority illusion" or the "Lake Wobegon effect." Ask a person how they rate themselves on any positive trait or task and odds are they will give themselves a seven or above. To be honest, I am probably not as self-aware as I believe myself to be. Knowing that my self-awareness could use refreshing, I decided to look deeper into distinct types of self-awareness. Dr. Tasha Eurich, a psychologist, conducted an extensive scientific study of self-awareness. The research included ten independent studies with approximately five thousand participants. In this study, the researchers found that there were two main types of self-awareness.

Internal self-awareness defines how we see ourselves, including our values, desires, ambitions, how we fit into our environment, and how our reactions (e.g., behaviors, thoughts, feelings, strengths, and weaknesses) affect others. On the contrary, when we lack internal self-awareness, we can experience anxiety, stress, and depression.

External self-awareness is our ability to perceive how others see us accurately. It is important to note that our level of self-esteem plays a key role in external self-awareness. If we have low self-worth, we are less welcoming to how others see us. External self-awareness recognizes what others see in us concerning our values, desires, and ambitions. It also sees others' views in terms of how we fit into our environment and how our reactions (including behaviors, thoughts, feelings, strengths, and weaknesses) affect others. The better we are at external self-awareness, the easier it is to show empathy—and we are open to others' perspectives. When we can see ourselves the way another does, it leads to more satisfying relationships and leaves space for our growth. Dr. Eurich's research found that people with high self-awareness in both types experience greater life satisfaction.

For most of my life, I was detached from seeing myself through the eyes of others. Why? I believed it would be too painful. I resisted taking the risk. Due to the trauma of childhood bullying, I thought that all people viewed me how the bullies saw me.

Not understanding that people's pain causes others' pain and not understanding my lack of internal self-awareness, the ridicule's repetitive nature became proof that the bullies' opinions were the truth. A child who continually hears "You are . . ." with negative labels like stupid, fat, ugly, and worthless attached can struggle with external self-awareness into adulthood.

My resistance to external self-awareness came from developing a sense of self through a traumatic experience. I am aware that my external self-awareness requires my attention, compassion, and a focus on growth. To home in on your level of internal and external self-awareness, you can answer the questions below.

QUESTIONS TO ACCESS YOUR SELF-AWARENESS

Internal Self-Awareness

1. Are you clear on who you are and what you want?
2. Do you regularly challenge your thoughts, behaviors, and views?
3. Do you accept your strengths and weaknesses without shame or judgment?
4. Are you aware of and work to heal past trauma?
5. Are you comfortable in your skin?
6. Are you able to stabilize yourself before a disruptive emotional reaction?

External Self-Awareness

1. Do you welcome outside feedback that points out your blind spots?
2. Are you open to different perspectives without the need to invalidate or argue?
3. Do you allow external viewpoints without overly worrying or altering who you are and what you value to please others?
4. Are you able to build healthy relationships with others?
5. Do you fear what others think of you?

(The more Yes responses you have, the better your level of self-awareness.)

Benefits of Self-Awareness

When our internal and external self-awareness is high and there is a balance between the two, we are more satisfied in life. What are some specific benefits of strong self-awareness? We worry less; therefore, we feel less anxious. When we understand our thoughts, bodily responses, and reactions, we can take proper action to avert burnout, redirect thought patterns, and respond to stimuli in more efficient ways. When we are self-aware, we have **enhanced self-confidence**. When we know what we are great at, we can navigate our lives, focusing on the best of us. Knowing our limits gives us permission to set boundaries and see areas where we can grow.

Self-awareness leads to a **deeper connection** with us and with others. When we are comfortable with vulnerability and talk to others about who we are, we open space for others to reveal themselves to us. Our willingness to hear others' perspectives creates less preconception in relationships, and we make a wider communication area.

Growth: When we pay attention to which thoughts serve us and which ones do not, we allow ourselves to create new thoughts. When we are focused on bringing about change and growth, change and development will follow.

Happiness: When we know ourselves, we understand what makes us happy. Knowing what makes us happy creates a drive inside most humans to seek out, change, and rearrange what needs to be done to reach our happiness.

Self-awareness seems like it would be a natural state of being, yet it requires a conscious decision to observe our thoughts, emotions, feelings, and behaviors. There are many advantages to self-awareness. So, how can we begin to realize the benefits?

Enhancing Our Self-Awareness

Get real with yourself. Admit you may not be as self-aware as you think you are. There's no shame here; I am right there with you on this one. Be open to learning by saying to yourself, "I don't know all that I need to know about myself, and I am willing to learn."

Mind your thoughts. Just like scrolling aimlessly through a social media feed, our thoughts are continuous and automatic. As does our breathing, our thoughts happen automatically—and most of the time without our direction. Unlike our breathing, which is necessary for our survival, most of our thoughts are unnecessary and not needed for survival. When we commit to improving self-awareness, we must mind the thoughts we choose to click on and follow.

Prioritize introspection. Carve out time each day to check in with yourself. How are you feeling? Why is your body responding to a particular situation? What was triggering about that event? One way I prioritize introspection is by journaling every morning. I created the Empath Morning Ritual Journal to meet this daily need for me, and I share it with everyone who wants it. You can request it on my website (www.realizedempath.com).

Welcome input. Begin the practice of welcoming outside feedback. Ask someone you trust to share how they see you. Be mindful of what feelings come up prior to asking, while you are asking, and after you ask. Make this practice a regular occurrence to strengthen your external self-awareness muscle. If this task feels scary to you, start with those you feel safe with and slowly challenge yourself to move outside your comfort zone. Remember this: You are love. You are worth. You are whole.

Cultivate stillness. Include moments of stillness and silence into your day. When we regularly quiet our minds and environments, we develop our ability to quiet our minds throughout the day and during times of stress. When we cultivate quieting our minds, we are more able to notice what thoughts come up in the present moment.

Allow space to respond. Give yourself time and space between your emotions and your reaction to the feeling. When you experience an emotion and it is clear you are triggered, allow yourself time before you react. This space allows for introspection and identifying a pattern of thought and reactive behavior. Giving yourself the freedom to go within enables you to choose a different response and break unhealthy habits.

Know your strengths. Years ago, I was yearning for change and a deeper connection to myself. One thing that helped me weed out all the negative commentary I had received from my actual strengths and value was taking the Myers-Briggs Type Indicator® assessment and the Clifton StrengthsFinder. These assessments were so beneficial for me, I encouraged my children to take the youth versions. You can find both assessments by performing an Internet search for Clifton StrengthsFinder and Myers-Briggs personality assessment. After taking these, I realized that I believed some of my strengths were a weakness; and the added self-awareness I received helped my confidence moving forward.

Be conscious of your distractions. What are your top distractions? When you are overwhelmed or anxious, where do you go, and what do you do? Are you pushing your feelings down with food? Do you have a specific nervous tick that surfaces during stress? Do you use sleep or television to avoid tough days, or are you prone to endlessly scrolling through social media?

Distraction is not always of concern, but obsessively escaping reality is pointing us to something within us that needs our attention. When we focus our awareness on our distractions, we can connect more deeply to our inner state and needs.

Know what bothers you. What complaints do you have about others that are repetitive and seem to be common complaints about various people? Notice the commonality in your protests and be open to the idea that what we refuse to see and heal in ourselves we project onto others.

The relationship between feeling resentment toward someone and our lack of boundaries is a splendid example. The higher your resentment levels, the weaker your communicated limits. If you make a list of all the people you resent and why you resent them, the list will show you your boundaries' health. When someone does something that upsets us, it is our responsibility to communicate, set a boundary, and follow through on that boundary. Often, the other person does the thing we are not okay with, we do not say anything, the person does it again, and resentment begins. As the behavior stays, our resentment grows until, eventually, we blow up or end the relationship, blaming the person for not knowing better or being a toxic person. Our lack of boundaries is what creates our elevated levels of resentment.

Take safe risks. I am the first one to say I would rather not attend that event of two hundred people. But taking healthy risks is a way we can strengthen our self-awareness and bring unexpected beauty into our lives. When we put ourselves in a new situation, outside our comfort zone, we allow ourselves to see something new about ourselves and experience ourselves through a different lens, which opens us to unique personal insight.

Evaluate your inner circle. Our relationship with ourselves can negatively affect our self-awareness, as can our relationships with others. Look at your most intimate relationships, including family. Can you express yourself without negative backlash? Are your accomplishments celebrated? Can you communicate constructive feed-back without punishment? Do your relationships have healthy boundaries? Are your relationships a mutual energy exchange, or are they out of balance? Do you have people around you that build your self-esteem but aren't in it for mutual growth and progress? Our innermost circle can adversely affect our self-awareness, and it is our responsibility to access and make a change when needed.

"

When self-awareness and
empathy join, our personal and
group power expand.

Group Self-Awareness

When we are not doing well in our surroundings, do we look at ourselves or look at our environment? Do we seek out our weaknesses and solely blame ourselves, or do we assess whether our surroundings are conducive to our strengths? When someone is not flourishing, the art of focusing on growing self-awareness and cultivating an empathic environment is healing and transformative for everyone. A family or societal structure that prioritizes self-awareness and empathy understands, values, and celebrates differences.

When a person regularly struggles within a specific environment, it is common for the blame to be on the individual without considering what other factors may contribute to their strife. For example, let us say that the person in this situation is highly perceptive, prioritizes the discussion of feelings, and likes to take their time to process information. They feel extremely uncomfortable being rushed and struggle in loud environments, surrounded by overly excited people. In this circumstance, it is common to look at the person who struggles but not at the entire family or system. The entire system will benefit from self-awareness development, and the group's self-awareness will create a healthy environment where all can thrive.

Self-awareness is the understanding of our nature, feelings, intentions, and desires. Empathy is our ability to listen, understand, and receive another person's experiences and emotions. When a family system lacks cohesiveness and members struggle to communicate, the environment is not growth focused and will struggle to survive. All families are made up of unique individuals with diverse needs and requirements to thrive. If the family members lack self-awareness, they will lack the ability to recognize what they need; and the group will lack the ability to empathize with each other.

On the other side, when we become aware of who they are and what we want, we start to see how we are alike—and our differences become transparent. This is where empathy flows. Understanding the benefits each person brings to the table and what it takes for each to thrive allows for connection and discussion and to remain focused on growth. If the family above has members who shut down feelings or are prone to raising their voices, improving everyone's self-awareness would help the other members gain insight into how they feel and how their needs are different. When self-awareness and empathy join, our personal and group power expand. The two can work together and directly affect the health and success of individuals and groups.

Self-Awareness Exercises

IDENTIFY YOUR ABCS

ABCs stands for:

A—Activating experience that triggered your inner dialogue

B—Belief after the event

C—Consequences or how you feel because of the belief

This exercise is excellent after you have experienced a difficult situation. Recording your ABCs helps you sort through the event and soothe yourself by reflecting and discovering what thoughts and beliefs came from the experience. When we sort through our inner and outer reactions to events, we gain insight into our stress response and better recognize our automatic thought patterns. Only when we see the automated nature of our thinking can we redirect our thoughts differently. Though many of us can experience the same stressful event, how we think about the event has a powerful influence on our lives.

Let us say you are on your way to work, and the freeway is moving slowly due to an accident. Your morning meeting is at 8 a.m. sharp, and you are worried you may be late. Do you become anxious at the thought of walking into the meeting late and take it out on the drivers around you? Or do you put your audiobook on and catch up while you wait?

No matter your choice, "A" stays the same, and "B" and "C" show you your stress response. This exercise helps us gain self-awareness of our automatic stress response, allowing us to make positive changes that benefit our bodies and minds.

CREATE A BUCKET LIST

Creating a bucket list helps you distinguish your personal and professional goals. Remember, self-awareness is about knowing what we want and desire. You know the feeling, the unconsciousness of obligational routine; we can lose connection to what we want.

SOUL ROAD MAP

Who said building self-awareness could not be fun? The Soul Road Map puts that notion to rest. Creating this is a simple and efficient way to help you understand where you could redirect some of your energy. The three parts of the Soul Road Map are **skill**, **fun**, and **need**. Skill refers to what you are naturally good at doing. What were you good at even before going to school or studying a trade? The fun piece is what you wish you could do all the time. What would you be doing if money were not a factor? Need is what the world needs, would pay for, and wants.

Creating this map will help you identify where you should focus, so you have a better chance of progress.

WRITE YOUR EULOGY

This task can be difficult for those who struggle with external self-awareness. To get the writing juices flowing, answer questions like the following: What do I want people to say about me at my funeral? How do I want to be remembered? What will people say about me now that I have passed on?

Doing this exercise will clarify what you would like to change in your life and where you would like to redirect your attention. It can also help you gain insight into how your reactions and choices affect those around you. Due to their sharpened sensitivity to emotional and physical energy, it is common for empaths to take on others' emotions without realizing it. Empaths will directly mirror another's feelings as though they were their own, and they may have a tough time differentiating their emotions and feelings from another.

"

Self-awareness is an essential
ingredient for an empath to
create a life that serves them;
self-awareness empowers
them to develop a lifestyle on
their terms.

Empaths can lose themselves in others' emotions. They can find it difficult to distance themselves from those who suffer even when it is in their best interest. Many empaths feel a displaced responsibility to save the world. Believing they are the only ones who can help, empaths tend to prioritize others' needs over their own. When they prioritize others' needs over their own, it is at the expense of their physical and mental well-being. Research confirms low external self-awareness has empaths prioritizing others' needs over their own, leading to depression and anxiety symptoms. For empaths, it can feel natural to put someone else's feelings above theirs, but it is harmful. They must be mindful of their limits and leave time each day to care for themselves.

Emotional intelligence requires giving empathy and compassion to ourselves. Even though it feels like second nature to offer support to others, empaths have to accept that they need comfort and attention and allow themselves and others to give to them. When they are self-aware, they will notice when an interaction goes from manageable to draining. In this scenario, it is not the other person's responsibility to change their energy. It is the empath's responsibility to meet their own needs. Reflect and ask yourself, "Am I taking on the feelings, moods, or problems in this conversation? Am I breathing deeply? What do I need right now?" As you become more aware of your needs, pay attention to the fear stories your mind tells you that hold you apart from meeting your needs—fear statements like "It's rude to ask to pause our conversation," "She won't love me if I stop prioritizing her needs over mine," "I've asked for support before, and no one showed up for me," and "Who am I to set a boundary?"

Empathy is a human practice. It hears the suffering in a neighbor's voice, listens attentively, and offers a supportive "I hear you." Reworded, empathy is a human practice. It is hearing the suffering in our inner voice, listening attentively, and offering a supportive "I hear you" and "I will act." Self-awareness is being conscious of what you need and being courageous enough to take action. Self-awareness is one of the most potent allies for our growth and transformation, yet only 10 to 15 percent of us are self-aware. When we lack self-awareness, we struggle in many areas of our lives because our thoughts, emotions, and behaviors affect us and others. When we achieve self-awareness, we know ourselves to the point where we consciously decide what we think, feel, and want to do. Self-awareness is an essential ingredient for an empath to create a life that serves them; self-awareness empowers them to develop a lifestyle on their terms. Having a lifestyle that acknowledges their sensitive needs enables them to rise fully into their strength and power.

ch 6   MENTAL RESILIENCE

Mental or psychological resilience is the ability to experience a problematic situation and bounce back from hardship.

Resilience is a mental strength reserve that one can access when confronting adversity. If we are mentally resilient, then we believe in our capacity to overcome and know the importance of not being engulfed by our experience. The difficulties of life are unavoidable, and sometimes the downs are downright awful. Enduring difficulty is something all humans encounter, but how we manage our setbacks plays an essential role in our ongoing health and happiness.

Have you questioned the frequency in which you are overwhelmed? Have you ever wondered if feeling so much without retreat is your fate? When we have mental resilience, we tap into our ability to cope and heal from trials and tribulations. People with mental resilience are not beyond the pain and suffering of the human experience. They, instead, depend on mental toughness to navigate their challenges. Mental resilience focuses on the acceptance of struggle and a belief in personal power. The absence of resilience revolves around victimhood and unhealthy coping mechanisms. When we lack resilience, we avoid our problems and require more time to bounce back. When we use resilience, we recover more quickly because we believe in the benefits of managing life's challenges as they appear.

When we have mental resilience, we are not looking at our challenges and forcing a positive outlook. We, instead, acknowledge the setback and accept that life comes with an array of experiences and that some of those are painful. Resilience is not the elimination of trials but the belief in our ability to handle them. A fantastic example of mental resilience is the story of a young girl from Pakistan who was shot in the head by the Taliban while riding a bus from school. Malala Yousafzai, unlike the Taliban, believed girls should receive an education; and the Taliban nearly killed her for her beliefs. This incident would be traumatizing for any of us, and I am confident Malala had a substantial share of fear and despair to sort through. It is what Malala did after the shooting that speaks well of her mental resilience. The tragedy strengthened her beliefs in the importance of education, and the violence was the recognition that changes needed to occur around the world. Malala continued with her passion for educating girls after the horrific incident and won the Nobel Peace Prize in 2014. Even when we are up against circumstances that seem incomprehensible, it is our resilience that garners us the strength not just to survive but to thrive.

Empaths and Resilience

Empaths are sensitive to all experiences, sight, scent, touch, smell, and body language. They uniquely tune in to the emotions and energy happening all around them. For a good part of my life, I thought the magnitude of what I sensed and felt was about me. The angst, the irritation, the hesitation, the shifts of energy, the hidden grief, the energy that did not match the words—I thought it was my presence, due to who I was. Before I understood why I experienced the world as I did, I spent my days overwhelmed. Can you remember the last time you were out in public and did not know how to continue with a task, so you looked around for silent guidance? Maybe you were at the library and were not sure about self-checkout, so you watched others for direction. As a child, I looked around and found no guidance for my most urgent task: How do I minimize and cope with everything coming at me?

As a young empath, I watched and had conversations with others. I noticed they were not aware of what I was sensing. They seemed unfazed. The world that affected me so profoundly was living their lives unconcerned. They either had some strength I did not have, they were excellent at pretending and therefore untrustworthy to me, or—the easiest one to accept—I was broken. When an empath or highly sensitive person decides they are fundamentally flawed, they cut themselves off from the idea of self-care. When we believe ourselves unworthy, we assume nurturing the brokenness does not change anything. The answer will appear in the changing of who we are; changing us will bring peace.

An empath who does not understand their experience can lack the skills to cope. When we do not know who we are, we will not care for ourselves the way we need. When we do not accept who we are, we will not take accountability to nurture ourselves the way we need. By the time I was a teen, I was overwhelmed by my existence. It felt like I was in a constant state of emergency. I was unsure how to lighten my load, I lacked trust in myself and others, and I was terrified of what I would feel next. I felt alone in my experience, fearful of human behavior; and I was convinced that life would be better if God would answer my prayer and change everything about me.

Empaths are inundated with their and others' energy and emotions every day. At first, they may try to be strong and soldier on. They make countless attempts at not being affected. They resort to acting like they are not affected by what they feel. Without avail, they give the "think positively" and "it's not how you feel but how you look" the good ol' college try. But eventually, they accept that overwhelm is normal and conclude there is no way out. They begin to accept that they cannot change their lives, and they stop any attempts to soothe themselves and make themselves feel safe. They believe their life and experience is unmanageable, and resilience comes from exposure to challenging but manageable experiences.

A child feeling consistently safe, understood, and cherished is largely related to how they will manage life's difficulties. As mentioned in nearly all resilience research in the last fifty years, the quality of our close personal relationships, especially with grown-ups and caregivers and social connectedness, is a critical part of human adaption. The young, mostly overwhelmed empath above will grow into an adult empath who lacks the mental resilience to overcome stressors efficiently. Without mental resilience, an empath will feel as if under attack each time of experiencing a room's heavy energy. Without mental resilience, an empath will take weeks or longer to recover from heavy emotions and energy. Without mental resilience, an empath will resort to unhealthy coping, isolation, avoidance, distraction, and blame. An overwhelmed and under-resilient empath will experience trauma-related symptoms like post-traumatic stress disorder, anxiety, adrenal fatigue, and depression.

Although our early experiences sculpt our brain and affect our mental strength, we can learn new ways to cope today and overwrite yesterday's programming. How we manage our stressors depends on what is in our resilience toolbox. Once we know what is in our toolbox, we can take what is not working and replace it with something that makes us feel safe, strong, and capable.

RESILIENCE BUILDING

You can think of resilience as an assortment of skills that can often be acquired. We can learn them as children or struggle into adulthood and learn them when we have reached a breaking point. Before we develop our new resilience skills, let us identify some coping tools that can hinder resilience building.

Drugs, drinking, overeating, gambling, shopping, and excessive screen time are some ways people cope with intense emotional experience. We pick up survival mechanisms to aid us in dealing with overwhelming emotions and trauma. Most of our disempowering coping practices stem from early life. Trauma can stunt our emotional maturity development. Adults may not model empowering coping practices, and lack of social support and isolation all hinder resilience.

COPING MECHANISMS

Apart from using my phone to disconnect from difficult feelings, my go-to coping mechanisms varied from year to year and included oversleeping, over- and under-eating, isolation, detachment from self, and switching between over-functioning and under-functioning. Identifying your coping mechanisms is not to shame or judge yourself; after all, we do what we believe we must do to survive. Not attaching shame or judgment might be tricky, since we live in a world that sees those attempting to cope as flawed. Remember, you are not inept; you acquired an unreliable way to manage trauma. Our purpose in identifying our coping strategies is to use them as notification for redirection.

For example, overwhelm can sneak up on me. I will not realize it until I have canceled my Thursday plans with friends or am sleeping hours past my alarm. I use my old coping patterns as a flag to direct me to internal assessment. When I feel like canceling plans, am I tired and need rest? Therefore, there's no need to dive deeper. Or do I feel like canceling plans because I watched the news and the country's state weighs on me? Have I given myself the attention I need to get through the complicated feelings, or am I isolating and sleeping to avoid the heavy emotions? Remember, when we fully know ourselves, we can care for ourselves the way we need to.

BENEFITS OF RESILIENCE

Coping healthfully with our stressors has many benefits. Our level of resilience aids in protecting us from various mental health concerns like anxiety and depression. The strengthening of mental resilience can help offset difficult circumstances that lead to mental health difficulties. When we are resilient, we can bounce back. Yes, we are struggling. Yes, it sucks; but we are solution-focused instead of blaming. The benefit of bouncing back is that we lose less time and momentum; therefore, we are achieving more of what we desire.

As we tap into our resilience reserves, we grow in our courage. In our reaction to our difficulties, we can choose helplessness or optimism. We always have the choice to move forward, focused on growth or collapse; run; or explode. The difference is courage. The work of not only seeing and honoring our suffering but making the best choice to move through builds connection. When we have the ability through self-awareness to show ourselves compassion, respect, and self-trust, we deepen our connection to our body, mind, and spirit. When we grow in harmony with ourselves, we can grow in connection with others.

When we are confident in our ability to bounce back, we take more chances; therefore, we live a more vibrant life. When we understand that failing is part of the human experience, we accept that new job. We start that new business, paint that painting, publish that story, or move to the new country. We take on meaningful hurdles to enhance our lives. Resilience and self-awareness come hand in hand, and the person with mental resilience knows when it is time to give up and move on. They can feel the inner tug of needed change or the cramped feeling of hitting the ceiling. Resilience allows us not to overstay our comfort zone and gives us the strength necessary for uncomfortable growth.

"

When we are confident in our
ability to bounce back, we take
more chances; therefore, we
live a more vibrant life.

CHARACTERISTICS OF RESILIENCE

The foundation of resilience is self-trust and a belief in something bigger than us. Resilience means that we do not let misfortune define us. We find our strength by inching toward a purpose beyond us. We move through pain by seeing tough times as a temporary stop on our journey. If trusting ourselves to prevail does not come easy, we can strengthen our belief in ourselves and see ourselves as sufficient and capable. It is possible to develop resilience. So, how do we develop the ability to rebound from our emotions? How can some people handle heavy energy and feelings and others shrink away and crumble?

Here are eleven common characteristics of people with high emotional resilience.

1. They have a belief in something bigger than themselves. Research shows that a commitment to a higher cause or a belief in something bigger than ourselves not only has a resilience-expansion effect but magnifies our thinking flexibility. Going round and round about something we cannot control has a detrimental impact on our ability to cope. Most resilient people have a heightened ability to accept things they cannot change about a situation.

2. They have a meaningful purpose in life. They have concern for others and are committed to a meaning for their existence, remembering this gives them courage and strength.

3. They strive to be a glass-half-full person. They look for the light in the bleak.

4. They take breaks from inside their head. They have a stillness practice—meditation, a walk in nature, journaling, art. They find reprieve in getting separation from their thoughts.

5. They ask for help (and most empaths said, "Ahh"). The most resilient among us know how and when to ask for help. They know which ones to call upon and which ones to avoid. Our most trustworthy confidants know how to shed light on our blind spots and direct us to a brighter path.

6. They prioritize self-care. The resilient have a nonnegotiable list of self-care habits. They know who they are and when care is needed. They do not skip meeting their well-being needs.

7. They admit (if only to themselves) that they do not have all the answers. When we are continually searching for solutions or believe others have the answers, we disconnect from our own psyche's innate ability to regulate stress.

8. They practice patience. The resilient often remind themselves that things happen on the soul's time, not their time. If we remove the concept of time and remember we are eternal, it can be easier to settle into the idea of patience.

9. They live in the moment. Staying present diminishes struggles of the past and fear of the future, allowing us to escape from adversity and conserve our inner energy.

10. They act with intention. Despite our grandest struggle, it is our responsibility to stay connected to our highest intention. Resilient people become the highest version of themselves by taking calculated risks consistent with their core intention.

11. They take responsibility. It is important for us to take responsibility for our actions despite the outcome or consequences. We must also be open to forgive self and others.

Some researchers speculate that resilience is an innate trait that people have or do not have. At the same time, other research suggests resilience is the combination of individual characteristics, attitudes, and behaviors all affected by environmental factors. It is the latter. We have the power to change our brains and alter the way we mentally process and bounce back from demanding situations. An escape from adversity is not attainable, but in identifying our specific challenges and discovering more productive ways to navigate them, we can drastically change the experience of our challenges.

WHAT HINDERS RESILIENCE?

A few months back, my husband and I took our children to a zip-line and ropes course. This place offered courses with various difficulty levels and heights. The young employee gave us a quick training, fit us for our helmet and gloves, and set us free to complete the two-hour adventure on our own. Our kids chose level six, the highest level. We had to use a unique key to access our area, which kept younger kids from entering this challenging level. I did well during the course, minus the occasional scream, elevated heart rate, and many pauses before stepping out onto a tiny rope one hundred feet (30.5 m) above the ground. Then I arrived at the last obstacle of the day; I zip-lined over to a tree canopy fifty feet (15.2 m) in the air. Once on the tree platform, I had a choice to make. I could take a more effortless way down or connect my harness to a pulley and jump off the tree platform. If working correctly, I would jump and the pulley would recognize my weight and gently drop me to the ground. My son walked up, connected himself, and jumped. The pulley came back up, and my husband attached himself and jumped. All of this is happening while I am breathing through my fear. Our daughter now begins to mock me, sharing her dislike of my anxiety and telling me how ridiculous I am being. My mind is swirling. Isn't it crazy to trust this pulley? Is it properly maintained? Where is the ladder? What injuries will I have if I hit the ground? Who is going to do my job(s) when I am in the hospital? I connect my harness to the pulley, check the connection a few times, sit on the platform's edge for two more minutes, and then ease myself slowly off the platform.

Being resilient does not mean we will not experience distress. In fact, the journey to resilience will include considerable emotional distress. Resilience is not a trait that people either have or do not have. It involves behaviors, thoughts, and actions that can be learned and developed by anyone. If tapping into our resilience is a possibility, what can cause some of us to give up or, like me, look for the easier route when the going gets tough?

Lack of social support: Did you know a lack of safe social connections is a risk factor for death? When compared with obesity and smoking, a lack of social relationships can kill us faster.

In a resilience article, the American Psychological Association pointed to many studies that show that the primary factor in resilience is having caring and supportive relationships within and outside the family. Relationships that build love and trust contribute to healthy role models that offer support and reassurance, helping bolster a person's resilience.

Extensive stress in childhood: A child experiencing prolonged stress or trauma is especially harmful. Extended trauma can affect relationship creation, including healthy attachments. A lack of quality connections creates feelings of not being safe, helplessness, and hopelessness; and excessive feelings of stress can create significant challenges for youth that can persist over time. Trauma often overwhelms a person's coping resources. Trauma can drive a person to find coping mechanisms that serve them in the short term but cause grave harm in the long term.

Stress-free childhood: A child parented to experience little or no adversity can lack resilience as well. Resilience appears in the presence of difficulty. When parents overly protect or solve their children's problems, the child can miss the opportunities to build self-trust and confidence to make it through a tough spot.

View of failure: Society frowns on failure, teaching us that we are either worthy (and therefore deserving of praise) or unworthy of any positive acknowledgment of our unworthiness. When we believe that stumbling means our unworthiness, we will avoid taking steps that risk a stumble. Redefining failure for ourselves and our children is a huge step forward for resilience building. Failure is not doing something wrong but not doing it at all.

Lack of body movement: Lack of exercise makes it more difficult for us to bounce back from stress. Exercise, sleep, good nutrition, rest, and meditation can all help suppress toxic levels of stress chemicals. Research has shown that regular exercise has a similar effect on mild to moderate depression to one popular antidepressant after one year.

Stressed nervous system: The autonomic nervous system brings us the fight, flight, or freeze response. Its function is reacting to our environment by igniting our mind-body reaction to a threat or maintain balance. Overuse of the autonomic nervous system's fight-or-flight response can harm our adrenal glands, making it more challenging to handle even the smaller stresses.

Resilience and the nervous system: The autonomic nervous system is fundamental to our resilience because it keeps us in the space of "handling it." A space of "handling it" is when our nervous system is calm, observant, engaged, and feeling grounded and balanced. When we are in this space, we notice, process, and respond to situations confidently. When we are "handling it," we can perceive, process, and respond to life events with calm composure. We can endure and be resilient.

If you step out of your comfort zone and attend a large social event alone, your autonomic nervous system will activate to help you face a challenge that feels scary. If you are attending the event with friends or had friends waiting for you, this event would feel less threatening because your brain's prefrontal cortex aids in regulation. When there are people nearby or tangible memories of people loving us, your prefrontal cortex can calm you through the social engagement system. Your prefrontal cortex's social engagement system is another example of how social connection is crucial to resilience. Being securely connected with others at the event or in memory allows one to notice, take necessary action, handle circumstances, and bounce back without overwhelming the autonomic nervous system.

Suppose you attend the event without friends and cannot tap into positive attachments or bonds from our past. In that case, you bypass your social engagement system, activating the sympathetic nervous system without any regulation. Now the space of "handling it" turns into fear, anxiety, and dread rather than rational, resilient responses. Returning to calm requires the activation of the parasympathetic nervous system, allowing you to return to a space of "handling it" to think calmly and respond skillfully. It is in this space that one can once again be resilient.

"

That is what a resilient empath is—a beautiful balance between sensitive and resilient, with the capacity to fully feel things but not be overwhelmed or dominated by what we feel.

Resilience Exercises

FEEL YOUR EMOTIONS

Sometimes, we get overcome for hours, even days, by our emotions. When our feelings hijack us, our feelings dysregulate us. The key to staying resilient is to allow the feelings to move through us without holding on to them. One way to remain emotionally regulated is to allow the emotion, even welcome it. Feel the emotion fully, with compassion, then meet the more solemn feeling you feel with a lighter emotion like gratitude or kindness, allowing both emotions to be present. As you allow the positive sentiment to grow within you, the more negative emotion will lose steam, positively affecting your brain and body's responses.

VAGAL NERVE STIMULATION

At the center of our bodies is a remarkably long nerve called the vagus nerve. It stretches from the brain down the chest and past the stomach. It attaches to our major organs, including ears, eyes, tongue, kidneys, bladder, reproductive organs, and the colon. Scientists believe the health of the vagus nerve affects anxiety and depression, blood pressure, and heart rate, as well as our digestion.

When we have an ideal vagal nerve tone, we are more resilient because we can more quickly shift with the help of our parasympathetic nervous system from an aroused state to a calm state. Long, deep breathing is a terrific way to activate the vagus nerve. Find a place to sit comfortably and close your eyes. As you inhale, pull your shoulders back and lift your head. As you exhale, loosen your jaw and relax. As you inhale, expand your belly with air. As you exhale, loosen and relax. As you inhale, allow the front and back of your rib cage to fill with air. As you exhale, soften and relax. Repeat for five to ten minutes.

Like breathing, singing can improve vagal tone. Research shows that professional singers have better heart rate variability and increased parasympathetic nervous system activity. If you want to make singing even more impactful to your resilience, do it while taking a cold shower. Research shows that cold exposure is another excellent way to stimulate the vagus nerve and your metabolism. Our heart rate, breathing, and stress level are firmly connected. When we get quality sleep, connect to our breath, and regularly move our body, we stimulate the vagus nerve. This means that establishing a self-care routine that includes rest, breath work, and exercise makes us not only smarter but more resilient and happier.

Sensitivity and resilience are two character traits that seem at odds with each other. When you think of sensitivity, do you think of someone who frequently feels intense emotions? When you feel more profoundly, you are more likely to be pulled into your body's stress responses. When you think of highly resilient people, you may envision someone who is unbothered by their circumstances and bounces back quickly from an emotional situation. Empaths' sensitivity describes how they notice and react to the emotions and subtleties all around them. For empaths, resilience is about responding to what they are feeling and how they perceive it. Being resilient is not due to a lack of difficult circumstances or never feeling intense emotions. An empath cannot escape complicated feelings, but they can embrace their strengths, care for their needs, and get to know their nervous system's workings to create more resilience in their life.

There were times I was inundated by others' emotions, and I felt like my body was stolen from me, leaving me frozen and buried under a weighted cloak. I remember years of feeling helpless, willing to do anything to make it stop. Resisting the magnitude of my experience, I would feel anxious, angry, and resentful. But most recently, I have noticed that the same level of emotions surrounds me; but I do not feel as engulfed. It is as if I have distance or space from the energy, even though it is all present. I still notice my level of comfort decrease and my body's response, but the space I have allows me to witness my reactions, tune in to my breath quickening, and see my mind race. Today I see my experience as an empath a bit more objectively, and I have allowed myself to prioritize well-being. When I notice heavy emotions or energy, I witness my body responding to the energy. I feel resilient, not because the experience is weaker but because I feel stronger. That is what a resilient empath is—a beautiful balance between sensitive and resilient, with the capacity to fully feel things but not be overwhelmed or dominated by what we feel.

GROUNDING MEDITATION SCRIPT

Find a comfortable place to sit, preferably where your back remains straight, your shoulders relaxed, and your feet flat on the floor. Close your eyes and take five deep breaths—in through your nose, out through your mouth. On your inhale, notice your belly filling up with air.

Returning to normal relaxed breathing, shift your attention to the ground beneath your feet. Take fifteen full breaths. With each exhale, feel the ground touching the soles of your feet.

Now gently shift your attention to your body in its entirety. Feel the space your body occupies in space and time. Notice what it feels like to be within your physical body at this moment. Sense all sensations your body has for you.

Return to your breath for another minute. Breathe deeply and mindfully, filling your belly with each inhale. Remain attuned to the sensations of your body. When you are ready, open your eyes.

ch 7 BOUNDARIES

Empaths can feel all that they feel and perceive all that they perceive and thrive without other people changing.

What they sense does not obligate them to entangle themselves with it. They are not bound to heal or repair anything outside of themselves. They may attempt to fix others, but they are not obligated. Their obligation in this life is to heal themselves. When empaths spend the bulk of their energy healing and fixing others and neglect themselves, they pay a substantial price.

Each of us has a limited amount of energy each day. If we spend most of our energy on others and save little for ourselves, we end up depleted, resentful, and suffering from symptoms that stem from a lack of physical and emotional self-care.

Having boundaries is an essential part of establishing your individuality and is a critical aspect of mental health and well-being. A boundary is where you begin and another person ends. It is a need rooted in self-awareness and a communicated limit that draws a line between being protected and wounded. A boundary is about taking care of yourself, not changing someone else's behavior.

Empaths cannot help but notice when others are in distress, and most often, they feel the pull to soothe others' discomfort. There are many benefits to empaths setting boundaries, including encouraging them to make decisions based on what is best for their well-being, not for those around them. This autonomy is a fundamental piece of self-care.

"

A boundary is about taking care of yourself, not changing someone else's behavior.

Why Do We Need Boundaries?

Setting boundaries has two objectives: (1) to protect ourselves from the infringe-ment of others and (2) to inform and remind ourselves of the space in which we begin to harm ourselves. The health of our boundaries corresponds to how well we know and accept ourselves. For years I allowed inappropriate behavior to go unchecked and un-communicated. For decades, I pushed myself past my breaking point instead of saying no or driving myself home—my need to be "liked" always overshadowed my need to be well. As I deepened my understanding of myself, showed myself compassion, and questioned falsehoods, I became more confident with my boundaries. Boundaries were embraced because I was worthy of feeling whole.

Every human comes with emotional pain, and depending on how aware we are of that pain, we will have coping mechanisms and behaviors that hurt others. Emotional pain and survival are a collective human experience and why boundaries are necessary. As we open to increased self-awareness, self-compassion, and self-care, we begin to understand our unhealed wounds and how they affect our behavior. Our unhealed emotional wounds, triggers, and reactions to them are why we and others need boundaries. Boundaries are a way of honoring humanity; healthy boundaries say, "I know you and I are both capable of healing, and I set this boundary to allow space for us to progress at our own pace." When we accept the human desire to heal, we all want to feel safe with our most profound pain; we can set boundaries from a place of commonality instead of judgment.

Empaths and Boundaries

Empaths are highly sensitive individuals who attune to the emotions and energy of others. It seems simple and, most times, automatic for them to take on the feelings of others. Going through life experiencing so much can be challenging when they lack boundaries and absorb others' pain and stress. For empaths, it is hard to ignore others' distress, and others' grief feels like their own to handle and dismantle. Like all humans, empaths want to limit the amount of time they suffer. Without boundaries, empaths can begin to avoid and blame others for their hurt. They are natural healers and want to see the world and those in it well, yet over-focusing on helping others can keep them from noticing their own needs and infringing on others'.

Being a natural healer and wanting to help others is a beautiful thing. Empaths are sharply intuitive and skilled at reading people and situations beyond surface-level interactions. Their boundaries are not about inhibiting the healer in them but honoring the whole of who they are and to prioritize their energy and needs. An empath's boundaries are not a way to shut out feeling but to feel and give themselves space to process and self-care to move beyond what they experience. Boundaries for empaths are not a separation from others or a wall built around them. Boundaries are not a lack of compassion or empathy, and they are not a way to isolate. Boundaries are self-care and self-love; they are an awareness of our unique needs allowing us to be the best version of ourselves.

TYPES OF BOUNDARIES

Boundary types vary. They can be physical, emotional, or energetic and can range from being relaxed to rigid. As we navigate our life and experience different things and heal emotional wounds, we will require various boundaries. Some boundaries may be set and never change, while others may be temporary or evolve when we grow.

Physical boundaries communicate what is and is not okay regarding your body and personal space. This boundary includes your physical needs like nourishment and rest and limits physical touch, like whether you are a hugger or not. Sexual boundaries would also fall under physical boundaries. One example of a physical boundary: When your manager at the restaurant you work at approaches you and rubs your shoulders, you step away, turn, and say, "I am not comfortable with that type of touch."

Emotional boundaries are empowering for empaths. They communicate the right to their feelings and emotions. They assert the necessity not to have their feelings criticized or invalidated. They also allow them to limit any expectations others might have about taking care of their feelings. Emotional boundaries say, "That is your feeling; this is mine."

Empaths need emotional boundaries for themselves, too. It can be easy for empaths to dive into the deep emotional end with people. An empath can refine their emotional boundaries to limit oversharing or diving too deep into subjects others are not ready to discuss. One example of an emotional boundary: "I am no longer comfortable discussing this topic. Let us change the subject."

Mental boundaries pertain to your right to have your own beliefs and opinions. When we have healthy mental boundaries, we can have discussions with others who have different views and not feel threatened nor belittle them for thinking differently than we do. Healthy mental boundaries allow us to hear opinions that differ from ours and not waiver in our belief system. Mental boundaries are limits for those who attempt to force their views upon us. One example of a mental boundary: Each time you express a belief or an opinion with someone, you are met with invalidation and belittling and left feeling silly for bringing it up. You can reply by saying, "I do not need you to agree with me, but in the future, I require a willingness to listen and show me a level of respect for my opinion."

Time boundaries are our responsibility to set limits with our time. How much time do you have for a phone call? How long can you stay at the party? If I have a one-hour session with a client, it ends at sixty minutes, even if discussing more would help. Our time boundaries go together with our level of self-awareness. How long can you stay at a party before you feel your energy draining? One example of a time boundary: "I would love to visit you over the summer. I cannot stay a full week, but I can stay for three days."

Material boundaries cover your right to use and protect your physical possessions, including money, as you choose. Following are two examples of a material boundary: "I am sorry, but I have made it a personal policy not to lend money to anyone;" or "I would prefer if you ate in the kitchen rather than sitting on my couch."

Energetic boundaries are boundaries established around the awareness of our energy. When we have healthy, energetic boundaries, we know exactly who we are, what we want, and what we align and do not align with. We are also conscious of our energy field and that which affects it. Remember the last time you attended an event or were around a specific person and felt your energy drain or noticed the effects after you left? Have you ever felt anxious or sad but did not know why? There is a good chance those around you were draining your energy without you or anyone else noticing.

Like our physical body, protected by our skin, our spirit has the defense of our energy. Every person has an energy field. This field is created by and for them, consisting of only their energy. Everything that exists has a field of energy surrounding it. The science of subtle anatomy calls this field of energy around us the "human energy field." The shield of energy surrounding us has various layers, with the outermost layer infiltrated more easily than the deeper layers. This energetic field or energetic boundary limits the amount of energy we pick up from others and curbs our energy field's penetration by someone else. Our protective energetic skin supports us by holding on to energy that sustains and resisting that which does not. When maintained and correctly managed, our energy field also attracts things that we require in our lives like guidance, healing, and relationships. We are born with clear and sound energetic boundaries. As we grow and endure dysfunctional family dynamics and traumatic experiences, the once secure connection we had to ourselves and how we see ourselves weakens.

When the water muddies around our values, needs, preferences, and talents, we will find it more challenging to prioritize our well-being over another. Unsure of ourselves, it becomes difficult to define what is right and true for us; and we find it challenging to know our responsibility from someone else's. When we detach from ourselves, we weaken our energetic boundaries. Some other ways we soften our boundaries are feeling accountable for someone else's life, shrinking ourselves to fit in, not speaking up, blaming others for our experience, and not realizing our value.

I detached from self-awareness and honoring myself early in life. By late elementary school, I had begun looking outside of myself for peace, acceptance, and to be told a positive account of who I was. As my energetic boundaries decayed, my behaviors became rooted in a desire to feel and experience my worthiness, such as:

- I continually pushed myself to a state of burnout.

- I would look for shortcuts, shortchanging my integrity because I was desperate for immediate feelings of worthiness.

- I would allow others to take from me emotionally, not requiring reciprocation.

- I would avoid speaking up and blame the other person's potential reaction for my silence.

- I would say yes when I wanted to say no and say no when I wanted to say yes.

- I would self-sabotage if those closest to me showed any sign of discomfort, jealousy, or negativity toward my growth and success. My success meant a loss of love.

As self-worth weakens, so do our energetic boundaries. Without a sense of energetic boundaries, we can unintentionally welcome things that do not serve us and resist the things we desire. Being unclear in our boundaries can have us experiencing anxiety, absorbing negativity, developing physical and mental illness, people-pleasing, in a constant state of overwhelm, and isolating ourselves out of fear. When we choose to only allow things that empower us into our energy field, we decide to show up being the whole loving being that we are. When we consciously decide what to allow, all else shall fall away—this is the universal flow of energy.

SIGNS YOU NEED BOUNDARIES

Maybe you know you need boundaries and you are navigating the challenge of setting them, or you are not confident in where and with whom you need them. An exercise I did years ago, and one I share with my clients, is The Resentment Test. Our resentments toward others directly correlate to the health of our boundaries. When we encounter a situation or behavior from someone we do not like, and instead of speaking up and setting a boundary, we judge, ignore the incident, and say things like "they should know better." We choose resentment over accountability. The behavior from them will continue, and we will continue to build resentment. In short, we are choosing the short-term discomfort of setting a boundary for long-term suffering of resentment.

Grab a piece of paper and write down each person or situation you resent. For added clarity, write down the behaviors or incidents that cause your continued resentment. What is important to understand is that the number of times they repeated the action you resent is not crucial to moving forward, because the repetitiveness is due to weak boundaries. What is important to recognize is what behavior(s) you need to set a limit around the next time they occur. Resentment harms those who resent, not those resented.

Signs You May Lack Personal Boundaries

- Being mistreated and not standing up for ourselves
- We give ourselves away to the point of physical and emotional exhaustion
- Shrinking physically, emotionally, and vocally to "fit in"
- Often feel we give without reciprocation
- Prioritize others' opinions over your own
- Overshare private details about yourself
- Seek constant validation and approval
- Feel responsible for others' happiness
- Regularly feel victimized

Signs We May Lack Energetic Boundaries

- Resentment toward feelings others' negative energy
- Often feeling overwhelmed by others' emotions and needs
- Out-of-the-blue feelings of negativity you cannot explain
- A sense of anxiety and need to be hypervigilant toward others' state of being
- People-pleasing in hopes to soothe someone's mood so you do not feel their negative energy
- Recurring relationship struggles
- Often feeling invisible or neglected

Remember, our boundaries protect us from being mistreated, and they communicate deep self-respect. They tell others what is and is not okay with you. They form a healthy physical, emotional, and energetic separation from others. Boundaries allow you to have your personal space, feelings, beliefs, wants, and views. They communicate the awareness you have about yourself and your needs rather than what others want from you. When we are in an empowered state, we establish our boundaries from an awareness of what we need to prosper. When we are in a state of long-term overwhelm, we can set boundaries from a place of resentment and survival.

Survival vs. Empowered Boundaries

When I recognized I needed boundaries, it was decades into my life and after years of built-up overwhelm and resentment. Like many of us living without boundaries, we grew up in families that did not model boundaries. Maybe, like me, you learned that your feelings were a burden; discussing pain meant losing attention (which I believed was love); or you suppressed your needs because you felt responsible for repairing adults' pain.

When I first acknowledged my need for boundaries, I held unhealed pain, resentment, and unspoken words. From this space, I implemented my first few boundaries as an act of survival. Setting these boundaries felt scary to me, laced with anger; but deep inside myself, I knew these initial boundaries would create the space I needed to heal. When we live most of our lives without boundaries and value others' needs over our own, implementing boundaries can feel like an assault on our emotional safety. As a child, I learned that I played an integral part in handling and healing adult's pain. Adults turned to me with their complaints and overwhelming emotions beyond my maturity and capacity to cope. I became the child who could soothe the adults but at the expense of my own needs, relationships, and well-being. Even as I write this, my mind teeters between fear and freedom. Putting words to my experience and expressing my pain risks hurting others' feelings and loss of attention.

For generations, my family has not spoken of the hurt we cause each other. We discuss with others but not each other; we create stories in our minds to remain victims. We tell ourselves we do not discuss it with the other due to their potential reaction, and if by chance we do mention how another hurt us, we risk feeling unheard and cut-off—and that feels like a loss of love. Setting my first few boundaries felt threatening, and due to how triggering it felt, I grappled with establishing them with kindness. Survival boundaries were a necessary part of my healing journey, but they were not a permanent stop. I knew to move forward, heal, and transform my life, I would need to take accountability. I had to take necessary action to heal, release resentment, and speak my truth to move from survival to boundaries rooted in self-love.

Empowered boundaries are less about controlling behavior and feeling less desperate, and are more rooted in self-love. A boundary stemming from self-love declares our right to be treated with respect and kindness. When we see our value and are mindful of the environments that enable our growth and well-being, we are more likely to see our rights to say no, change our mind, feel safe, have our thoughts and feelings, rest, and see our right to joy and peace. When setting boundaries, it is natural to experience fear. We may fear backlash, conflict, or loss of love. Fear may tell us that our limits will upset others, so we sacrifice our needs to "keep the peace." This state of discomfort will be temporary and declines with practice, or the distress can be consistent and intolerable when the fear derives from codependency.

CODEPENDENCY

Implementing boundaries can feel scary and awkward as we chart unexplored territory. It is normal to receive resistance from others and feel some inner struggle when setting boundaries in relationships that have not had them before. Though it is common to encounter discomfort, some of us will experience excessive distress, making it laborious to establish and uphold our boundaries. When we have codependent tendencies, we are more likely to absorb others' feelings and take responsibility for making them feel better or fixing their issues. Codependency is not related to our mental health; instead, it is a learned behavior, usually learned in early childhood. It is common for the child to have parents or other close adults who modeled codependent relationship dynamics. Often children are expected to take on adult responsibilities or mend adult problems. That child learns how to keep their needs hidden, put others' needs first, and observe the praise and adoration that comes with soothing a parent's feelings. When we mirror codependent behaviors, we do not cultivate self-worth nor see ourselves or our needs as a priority. Codependency blinds us to our needs and our separateness from others; if they suffer, we struggle. Codependency has us looking for someone to fix, tend to, or patch rather than finding an independent, stable partner or friend who takes 100 percent responsibility for their happiness.

Codependents, or what I sometimes call people pleasers, frequently choose friends and partners that continue the pattern of emptying their issues and heavy feelings on to them with little or no responsibility. In the codependent dynamic, we have one taking over accountability while the other takes the minimum or none. Codependency can complicate boundaries because boundaries require us to be assertive and prioritize ourselves and our needs. Struggling with codependency means we often wrestle with expressing ourselves due to fear of rejection and objection. It is common for someone with codependent tendencies to take no action to change a relationship but expect others to "know better," "read their mind," or sit back and hope things magically improve.

If, like me, you did not have boundaries modeled in childhood and you took on the responsibility of soothing your parents' pain, you may be quick to hold responsibility for things you have no control over or accept blame for something you do not do. Struggling with codependency means we concluded that we are responsible for what others do. We assumed our goal is to make others feel better. We settle upon believing our feelings are a burden; therefore, we are inadequate in not handling them ourselves. Boundaries are vital for healthy relationships in which both individuals have space to flourish. When a relationship has boundaries, both people are accountable for their feelings, thoughts, and behavior. If you struggle with boundaries and codependency, it will help you to clarify what you are responsible for in your relationships and what you are not.

Get a piece of paper and write down what you are responsible for in a relationship. For example: "I am responsible for what I say, not what they hear." "I am accountable for my feelings." "I know what is best for me, not them." "It is not my job to give unsolicited advice." It is imperative to know yourself, your values, needs, wants, and priorities. Deciphering what you are and are not responsible for is crucial to feeling comfortable setting boundaries and fostering healthy relationships.

It is a beautiful thing to offer help to our loved ones and those in need. Boundaries are not about building a wall around us and not extending support to those in need. However, if we give to others while having weak boundaries, we are more likely to feel over-responsible for their struggles and feelings and take full responsibility for fixing them. We do not give ourselves space to see our needs or allow others to step up and help themselves. Humans build self-love by putting themselves first, and we feel empowered when we act and the progress leads to desired change. We must remember that fixing someone else is not possible, nor does it lead to empowerment. Boundaries give room for our needs to matter and for theirs, too.

Boundary Reminders

Do you know you need boundaries, but you are unsure where to start or what to expect? Here are some reminders to guide you through the process of establishing your boundaries.

- It will feel awkward, and you may experience feelings like fear, anger, or even sadness. Feeling an array of emotions is normal, and it will get better with practice. Remind yourself why you are setting boundaries. Soothe yourself by recalling that boundaries are about loving and respecting yourself. You are worth it.

- When you get pushback—and you will—do not apologize, alter your boundary, or respond in anger. Take any pushback as proof the boundary was needed. Remember, you are not responsible for their reaction; you are responsible for respectfully communicating your boundary. Try not to take adverse reactions personally but do plan on it and for it. Be kind and assertive. Mixed messages lead to crossed boundaries.

- Setting boundaries takes practice and grace. Allow yourself the room to flounder but stand back up and keep at it. Do not let your fear prevent you from loving yourself.

- When you catch yourself in resentment mode, talking or complaining about others, you more than likely need to set a boundary. Be willing to use your behavior and feelings as a guide to see where boundaries are needed.

- The process of identifying the need for and establishing boundaries takes time. Give yourself the time, rest, reassurance, and support you require to take the plunge.

- As new relationships present themselves, remain self-aware and look for signs that the new person will appreciate and honor boundaries. Be accountable for any new relationship dynamics you allow and change or end any unhealthy connections you hold.

Remember that any step forward is still forward. Baby steps are as powerful and a huge step. Reach out for support and guidance when you need it, and like most things, practice is the difference between where you want to be and where you are now. Because I have codependency in my blood, boundary reminders were useful in soothing my fear. Another tool that helped ease anxiety and worry were boundary scripts. When being assertive with our needs and feelings feels unnatural, we can feel clumsy putting words together. A boundary script pairs an example social interaction with sample ways to respond. Although the specific situation may not be what you are experiencing, most times, you can alter a few words and make the example work for you.

"

Setting boundaries takes practice and grace. Allow yourself the room to flounder but stand back up and keep at it. Do not let your fear prevent you from loving yourself.

Boundary Scripts

You would like to set a boundary with a friend. In recent conversations, another friend's name comes up, and you find yourself listening and entertaining her complaints and judgments of this friend. After the interactions, you leave feeling discouraged, guilty, and drained.

On your next phone call with her, you say, "I know you are struggling with what happened between you and Kay. I, however, am not comfortable discussing Kay or the situation any longer." In future discussions mentioning Kay, you follow up by saying, "Remember when I told you that I was not comfortable discussing Kay? We will need to change the subject, or I will have to get off the phone." If your friend mentions Kay in future discussions, you remind her of your boundary or end the conversation.

Another scenario: Your mother tends to make comments about your weight or eating habits during family gatherings. During the next conversation with your mother, you say, "Mom, you have a habit of bringing up my body and diet when we are together. I am not comfortable with others discussing my body or how I nourish myself. In the future, can you please refrain from doing this?" If the topic returns, you remind her of the boundary and set the consequence. "Remember when I told you I wasn't comfortable with this topic? If this happens again, I will leave."

WAYS TO SAY NO

- I am not into XYZ, but thank you for thinking of me.

- I am not being guided to do that.

- Thanks for the offer, but I will pass.

- This is not feasible for me.

- Thanks, but I would rather not.

- I love that you asked me, but I cannot make it work.

- I am not able to maintain my responsibilities and attend, but thank you.

- I am unavailable this weekend.

- I am not able to meet your expectations around this. If you have the flexibility, we can discuss further.

- That is not a good fit for me at this time.

"

With boundaries, we dare to be
all of who we are instead of a
fraction of what is possible.

Energetic Boundary Script

Remember, energetic boundaries are about an awareness of yourself and how your energy feels in each moment. Energetic boundaries are boundaries we set for and with ourselves.

Your partner enters the kitchen and begins to tell you about a heated conversation with a coworker. As he continues into the story, his frustration and anger grow, and his energy begins to feel heavy. You notice that your body is reacting to his energy, and you begin to talk him out of his frustrations so you can feel better.

Use the following five steps as a way to create boundaries:

1. Take a mental step back and disengage your words and thoughts. Shift your attention from your partner's energy to yours. Do this by taking a deep breath and saying a word or a phrase that feels supportive and grounding. I like to say, "I'm safe" or, "This isn't my energy." Some find "Here I am" helpful.

2. Once you feel your focus return to you and your body, say your first name. Saying your first name helps you focus further on your experience.

3. Ask yourself, "Is this my emotion?" "Am I feeling this?" "Who's feeling this way?"

4. Next, put details on what happened. "My partner walked into the room and is sharing a stressful situation while showing frustration."

5. Last, describe some things that separate you from your partner, like "I am female," or "Today I am going to the gym," or "The shirt I am wearing is soft."

The goal with energetic boundaries is to remain centered in our energy, aware of what is ours and what is not, and take action to keep our peace. Boundaries guard us against mistreatment, and they communicate how others should treat us. When we have boundaries, we have a healthy separation between our physical body and emotions and others' emotions and body. Boundaries support us in having our thoughts, feelings, needs, ideas, privacy, and space. With boundaries, we dare to be all of who we are instead of a fraction of what is possible.

ch 8 NURTURING YOUR ENERGY

For most of my life, "Take care of myself" meant change myself.

If you had pulled a chair up beside me ten years ago and told me that self-care was the answer and if I cared for myself, it would lead to feeling how I wanted to feel, I would have rolled my eyes and wished you well. I had built my life on the notion that if I could morph myself enough—be more, be less, achieve, pretend I did not feel—I would attain the peace I desired. By the time I was eighteen, I had settled upon people being unsafe and acquired the survival mechanisms that continued a chain of misery.

We learn how to "survive" in the world by watching the adults around us. No child escapes picking up their parents' coping mechanisms. Our grandparents learn from their parents, continuing through generations until we wake up to the destruction and take accountability to heal and learn healthier ways to cope. Although we can have different coping mechanisms, excessive fixing, staying small, and withdrawing to remain safe have caused me suffering as an adult.

As you can see, these survival skills are in direct opposition to each other, creating an inner war within myself. I was taking one step forward with an immediate step back. I was dipping my toe into relationships, assessing, and pulling it out for most of my life. These ways of coping were what I knew—what was modeled and deeply ingrained in me. These behaviors felt familiar and safe, and I had adopted them without thought.

Before we are aware of our survival skills, we draw on them when we are emotionally overwhelmed, are triggered by our trauma, or do not feel safe (even if we are). As an empath, I engaged my survival mechanisms most of my life. I learned to use my empathic abilities to access risk. I accessed each person and categorized them into three categories: potential non-threat (therefore, offer help and do for them to earn my keep), potential threat (be kind but maintain distance), and danger (build a wall and keep them out). Once I categorized someone, it did not mean they always stayed in that category. I was continually reassessing to update my risk.

Sometimes it is our unhealed trauma that causes us to be hypervigilant. In my case, it was trauma paired with my ability to notice the most subtle hints of inauthenticity and the discrepancy between feelings and words. I did not know how to reconcile what I felt versus what people presented. If I shared something fabulous that was happening to me, and friends or family met me with a smile and a "that's great" but the energy radiating from them felt resistant, I would chalk it up to their inability to be happy for me and would deem them a threat. I never considered their unhealed trauma or pain—only how their energy was affecting me. It was not until I had a complete emotional and physical breakdown that I learned about empaths.

As I nursed and healed my trauma, it became clear there was another factor at play in the overwhelm I felt in my daily life. What caused my suffering was threefold: trauma, coping mechanism, and absorption of emotions and energy. What saved me was prioritizing self, self-care, and healing.

Self-Care

Empaths are highly attuned to the emotions and energies swirling around them. They are also hypersensitive to the effects this awareness has on them. When they witness intense emotions, they experience harsh after-effects. Maybe you've noticed you feel drained after attending an event, or you are like me and feel exhausted and emotionally charged after hearing others' struggles without recess. Self-care is the difference between an empath feeling they have no control of their experience and creating the life they want to experience. The best thing I did for myself was making self-care a lifestyle. Self-care became a nonnegotiable aspect of my everyday life. Done are the days of a once-a-year Mothers' Day massage. I am an empath, and the world I experience differs from other people. I have unique qualities and, therefore, unique needs; and self-care is how I provide myself the support I need to flourish.

Self-care can be anything that feels good to you. It changes as our needs change and can be anything from a private dance party to three minutes of breath work, a nighttime walk, rest, writing, connecting with friends, alone time, acupuncture, or standing up for yourself. We know how well our self-care practice is going by how good we feel.

* What will make you feel nourished this week?
* How do you want to feel?
* What inspires you?
* Be curious and have fun. What have you always wanted to try?

If you are like me, you prefer to try different things and mix things up. My non-negotiables are meditation, movement, writing, rest, and nature. Over the years, I sprinkle in when needed infrared saunas, red-light therapy, acupuncture, Reiki, cryotherapy, talk therapy, sound therapy, breath work, aromatherapy, and more. Your self-care practice is all about you. Design it to soothe your soul and give yourself the love you have always wanted.

"

Cultivating a loving,
trusting, and supportive
relationship with yourself
means prioritizing yourself.

EMPATH MORNING RITUAL

When empaths sleep, they let go of their past thoughts and energy. When they wake, their energy is fresh and aligned with their highest self—that is, until they think the thoughts they were thinking yesterday. The energy they wake with is their clearest and highest of the day, and they deserve to give that energy to themselves. Raise your hand if you have stayed up past your point of exhaustion to get "alone time." Keep your hand up if that alone time did not equate to actual quality time with yourself.

Cultivating a loving, trusting, and supportive relationship with yourself means prioritizing yourself. I would wake up and immediately begin the rush of tending to others' needs. That theme would continue until 8 p.m., when my trance turned to irritation and exhaustion. At that point, I would grab my phone or turn on the TV, emotionally distance myself from my family, and call it my time. I gifted myself time, but it was laced in depletion and detachment and last on my priorities list.

Today I give myself the most positive energy I have—my morning energy. When I wake, I take a moment before my thoughts begin and notice the space around me. As I become aware of my room, I remind myself of the things I love and appreciate. I say things like "These sheets are soft on my skin," "I love how the sun is filtering through the blinds," or "The cool breeze of the fan feels good." I give myself five full minutes of gratitude before I move on to brushing my teeth. Keeping my thoughts light, I move on to my Empath Morning Ritual Journal.

An empath's morning energy is fresh and closest to higher consciousness. Morning time is a beautiful opportunity to write in a journal. I use journaling to connect to my inner wisdom, access my deepest thoughts and stories, and see the more profound truth in any pain I am feeling. I put my journaling method in the Empath Morning Ritual Journal. It is available for you to download on my website (www.realizedempath.com). I journal to sort my feelings, plan my day, witness energy I am holding, and heal my pain.

Another wonderful way to stay grounded in our morning energy is meditation. Any type is perfect. I change my meditations based on my needs, how I want to feel, and what I am going through. If you are new to meditating, try some guided meditations. In guided meditation, another voice guides you into a relaxed meditative state. We go further into meditation later in the chapter.

Movement is something else I do in the morning if my energy demands it. If it does not happen at sunrise, I implement it later in my day. Energy wants to move, and empaths need to move the energy to feel their best. Movement is also essential for mental and physical health.

Your morning routine should feel right to you. Prioritize how you want to feel. Create whatever you desire and give yourself your most valuable morning energy. My most desired feeling is freedom; therefore, I provide myself with things that aid in my emotional liberation. I journal to release; I meditate, creating space to choose new reactions; and I move my body to clear myself of heavy energy. What do you need? What feels best and most supportive to you? Answer those questions, then give yourself that every morning.

THE POWER OF MEDITATION

One of the most meaningful gifts a highly attuned empath can give themselves is to meditate. You may come to meditation from a spiritual standpoint delving into what it means to be a higher being and learning the history of meditating and its significance to cultures worldwide. You may be more into proof and data, choosing to investigate the science of meditation and try because of the evidence; or you can come to it as I did—in desperation. Meditation was something I was ready to try because I was desperate for relief. I longed for time-outs from my thoughts. I craved an inner peace I knew existed but had not yet found. At first, meditation felt odd; I spent months waiting for something profound to happen. When was the big revelation going to arrive? Would I see a swirling bright magenta light and be drawn into consciousness? When would my mind shut up? Don't scratch the itch; stop thinking about scratching the itch; you scratched the itch—meditation fail.

I did not realize it then, but my noisy mind and racing thoughts were part of meditation. My persistent thoughts did not need to disappear for meditation to be of value. By surrendering to my thoughts and witnessing their presence without the force pulling me under, I would be free to choose different thoughts and select different reactions. Our ability to remain still among our thoughts is a skill aiding us in staying calm amid others' energy and emotions. These moments of stillness prioritized my need for inner and outer quiet, giving me freedom from the thoughts enslaving me to the same life experiences.

Your curiosity is vital when beginning a meditation practice. What are your needs today? Do you need increased energy, guidance, or healing? Look into different ways to meditate that speak to you today. Do you need to be uplifted or need help relaxing? There are meditation techniques that focus on the things you need. I started my meditation practice sitting down as you see in the movies, legs crossed and hands on my lap. As my curiosity and confidence grew, I realized I could have meditative inner silence with my eyes open, driving my car, walking in the yard, or writing this book. With this newfound strength, I could access inner peace wherever I was; and I was getting better at obtaining it around heavy energy. Meditation is our full presence in whatever we are doing. Are we at peace with the present moment? Can we follow our breath? Do we sense our body and all its sensations?

JOURNALING

I have years of journal pages. it is fascinating to read my journal from years ago and see how spirit guided me to greater insight, more profound healing, and increased self-awareness through writing. Empaths have feelings, and frequently those feelings are big. Journaling is an excellent way to process those big feelings and emotions. Journaling can turn what are believed to be hurt feelings about not being invited to a party into a deeper awareness of childhood pain, necessary healing, and eventually a loving understanding of ourselves.

A common desire of empaths is to feel heard and seen for all that they experience. Journaling gives them an expressive voice to expose all that they feel—their heartbreak, trauma, and stress—and express their joy and excitement. It is common for empaths to feel bombarded by their thoughts and feelings. Journaling allows them to tap into their intuition and return into themselves. What am I feeling? What thoughts am I thinking about what I am feeling? Maybe you'll start on a topic and sort through it for weeks in your journal, getting to a higher truth. Perhaps you will begin with a belief and quickly discern it as not factual. It is your journal. Express your spirit, untethered and unquestioned. It is what empaths all desire. It is healing.

Caring for ourselves means we want to reduce stress. We want to experience more moments of joy, and we know the importance of seeing our patterns of thought and behaviors that cause us harm. Research has proven that journaling offers ample benefits to our mental health, one of those being our ability to process our and others' emotions.

When we are overcome by what we feel, we can have trouble trying to walk ourselves out of the intensity using our mind. Journaling utilizes the brain's left side, the analytical and rational side. When we write, it frees up the brain's right side to feel, create, and tap intuition. Journaling serves as moments of self-reflection. It is an excellent way to slow down, be present, and process overstimulation. If I feel it, I write it. Putting it on paper has allowed me to sort through deep-rooted pain that followed me for decades. When we lighten the load we carry, we will be less affected by the new energy we perceive today. Permit yourself to stand in confidence with your truth—without outside validation, without watering it down—then clap for yourself.

Our Body

An empath's body is the vessel that carries all their emotions. When they feel sad, they may feel the energy in their chest. When they feel embarrassed, they may notice it in their throat or face. An empath who spent most of their life overcome by emotions might disconnect from their body, seeing their vessel as untrustworthy or choosing to numb their feelings through various means like food. An empath's ability to be present in their body and tend to its needs impacts the energy they perceive and how much energy they hold.

It takes tremendous energy to process emotions, and empaths sort feelings—whether theirs or someone else's—in the same energetic center (also referred to as chakra) that manages their digestion. When they have an emotionally full day, they use a substantial portion of our energy, equating to less energy to support their digestive system. Providing their body with the nourishment and movement it requires helps them process emotions, leading to the monumental shift many long for—feeling more empowered feeling others' energy and feelings.

Let me start by saying this: We are all different; there is no one-size-fits-all in nutrition. What works for you is what makes your body feels strong, light, and healthy; and your ability to notice how your body feels after food requires conscious attention. It is best to draw on your intuition, welcome curiosity, and question what others have told you to eat and believe. What makes your body feel its best? What emotional wounds do you hold that affect how you nourish your body? Do you eat to restrict and control? Is food about love and nourishment? What resistant thoughts come up when thinking about eating differently?

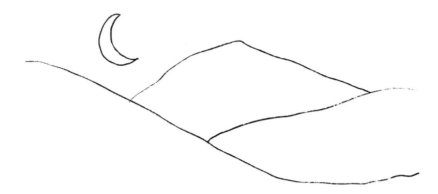

NOURISHMENT

If you are embarking on nutrition changes, keep a notebook. How do you feel an hour after each meal? What feelings come up? How is your body responding? Use your findings as a guide for eating the following day. For an empath, nutrition is a necessary tool, supporting their body in processing the increased emotions they encounter each day. I feel more supported in my body when I eat a warm soup than I do with a cold salad, even though society has been pushing salads since the 1980s.

I was utterly disconnected from my body for most of my life. I disregarded my body because it was the root of my pain. It is the place I felt the overpowering emotions and energy. I did not eat or move to love and nourish; I ate to numb feelings, restrict, and punish. Eating was never about care, and any "negative" response my body had was due to its failure, not to how I was supporting it. As I embarked on my journey of empath empowerment, I prioritized getting to know my body. What things does my body struggle to digest? Did I have any food allergies? What did a DNA test show me about my body?

As I prioritized my body, I noticed my sensitivity toward it grew. I confirmed my caffeine sensitivity through a DNA test, which I knew for years but chose to ignore. My body and mind felt heavier if I veered off from eating supportive foods. I become constipated very quickly when my stress levels are up, water intake is down, or protein levels are up.

Remember what works for my body will be different from yours. Think of this as a journey back to body connection. As you turn your loving gaze back to *your* body, what it requires becomes clear. What feels good to you and in you?

MOVEMENT

Science proves that exercise benefits are plentiful. Our body, mental health, spirit, and energy levels all profit from moving our bodies. When an empath moves their body, they get all those benefits and more.

• Moving the body aids in body connection and being grounded. Empaths spend a lot of time in their heads, so consciously connecting back to the body gives a much-needed reprieve.

• When the body is strong, it can better process the heavier emotions.

• Energy wants to move, and moving the body is a fantastic way to move and process that energy.

As disconnecting from the body leaves us not knowing how to nourish it, disconnection can also leave us not knowing how to move it.

Move your body in a way that feels good. I feel great when I dance to an inspiring song. I feel bored and in my head when I use a rowing machine. I feel connected and grateful when I am running in a beautiful park. It feels forced and disempowering to run on a treadmill. Listen and move your body how it desires and be flexible. How you move it today may be different from tomorrow. Remember, the intention is to support your body and the energy you carry, not whipping your vessel into shape.

Exercise has an element of grounding, which is essential for empaths' well-being. Grounding helps us eliminate excessive energy in the body, opening space for fresh energy to come through. When we are grounded, we are calmer, our emotions ease up, and we have a clearer view of our inner and outer world. Taking moments to ground ourselves helps us feel physically and emotionally balanced and less anxious.

Energy Protection

Everything is energy, including all thoughts and emotions. There is no better time than now to get cozy with the vital concept of energy. Most of us on any given day put ourselves in situations that drain our energy. The sheer act of thinking negative thoughts drains our energy. Although it is a popular pastime to blame others and their energy for affecting ours, it is our responsibility to protect and manage our energy. Protecting our energy comes in two categories: ongoing maintenance that keeps us strong, like nutrition and movement, and more defensive tools to utilize when we notice dense energy in a room. Some protection tools like meditation, minding your thoughts, and clearing your energy can be day-to-day and situation-based.

SHADOW WORK

If all thoughts and emotions are energy, then any past trauma we hold that is easily activated and affects our behavior drains a generous portion of our energy. We are not responsible for all our emotional wounds, but we are responsible for healing them. Taking accountability and the action required to recover is a massive step in protecting and preserving our energy. Shadow work can be energy draining, but the long-term payoff is undeniable.

ENERGETIC BOUNDARIES

An energetic boundary is a buffer or protective energy field made by you only and contains your energy. Creating these energy fields intends to keep your energy separate from others' negative energies but allow the exchange of positive and loving energies.

Following are three things make energetic boundaries possible:

1. Get familiar with your energy. Observe how your energy is affected in all situations. What drains you? What fills you? Be mindful of your thoughts and emotions; negative thoughts lower our energy. Prioritize self-care; a great starting point is utilizing the ideas in this book.

2. Accept that what you allow within your energy field is 100 percent your responsibility. Get clear on your intention for the boundary. The clearer you are, the more likely it is that you will get the results you want.

3. If you are not comfortable doing what is right for you, commit to seeing any emotional wounds affecting your self-esteem.

When we have energetic boundaries, we take full accountability for our energy and what we allow in and out. Our awareness of our bodies, minds, and energy in all situations helps us make deliberate choices and snap decisions that serve our energetic needs best.

CLEARING

Empaths notice and frequently absorb energies and emotions from people and circumstances every day. Some of what we notice offers us no personal benefit. That is why it is imperative to cleanse our energy fields frequently. By doing regular energy clearings, empaths can protect their energy field and help themselves stay grounded and clear minded.

Following are some simple ways to clear your energy:

Water: Submerge your body in a bath, lake, or ocean. Adding Epsom salts to your bath or using it as a scrub in the shower adds extra benefits.

Visualization: Wherever you are, visualize energetic arms extending out the bottom of your feet. See in your mind's eye the dense energy no longer serving you exiting your body and entering the earth. You can do this anywhere, with extra (grounding) bonus points if you do it barefoot on the grass or soil.

Unplugging: Take time away from energy-draining technology, loud noises, and news. Reallocate the energy you would spend back to you.

Meditation: Some great guided meditations focus on clearing energy. I have one on my website (www.realizedempath.com) for you and others.

SHIELDING

Research has proven the mind and body advantages of visualization. Several studies show that the brain cannot differentiate between a real and imagined event. This means that when we visualize something we desire, we create a memory, making the unknown known. When our brain registers the event as handled, we will experience less stress and anxiety around that thing we desire. Research also confirmed that visualization used by world-class athletes helps them develop skills faster. When they visualize actions, the same brain areas react as if they are performing them; therefore, they are training using their brain.

Shielding is visualizing and a simple way to protect your energy. We can use shielding to prevent lower vibrating energy from entering our energetic field while allowing love exchange.

You can do a shielding visualization an hour before you attend an event or do it as soon as you feel uncomfortable. Begin by taking a few deep breaths, in through your nose, out your mouth. Visualize a brilliant shield of light (any color that feels good to you) encircling your body, extending a few inches beyond. Set the intention that this shield of light will protect you from anything not serving your highest good. It is essential to access the emotions you feel when you feel protected and loved. Believe that this shield will block out negativity, and at the same time, you still sense what is positive and loving. Set an end time for your protection—if the event is an hour, ask for an hour.

MEDITATION

Everything is a form of energy. Whether we observe it or feel it, we wander through an overabundance of energy all day long. We create energy with each move we make, every thought we think, and every word we speak—even the things we do not do but should expel energy into the world. Meditation allows us to intentionally focus our attention on positive thoughts, emotions, and actions. If we allow it, meditation can connect our focus's power to visualizations and feelings that align us with higher energy. After meditation, we have cleansed energy; and our energy is a higher vibration.

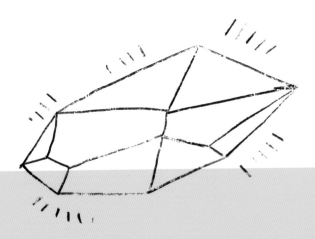

CRYSTALS

I love crystals. Going into a gem store is such a personal, almost private experience for me. I believe in the power of crystals and feel drawn to certain ones depending on my needs. Crystals are stunningly beautiful minerals, stones, and gemstones that many believe transmute, guard, and amplify different energies. I have some lying around my house, some on my bathroom vanity, clusters on my writing desk, many in my jewelry, and a large amethyst turned nightlight. If you have not visited a gem store, I highly suggest you do. Learning about each crystal while holding them will help you discover the perfect gem for you. Some of my favorites are the following:

Tourmaline: It is said to promote inspiration and happiness, reduce fear, and build self-confidence.

Amethyst: It is used for tranquility, grounding, and a sense of calm.

Fluorite: This crystal assists in spiritual sensitivity, creativity, growth, and transformation.

Obsidian: It supports our shadow work, more profound healing, and self-discovery.

Smoky quartz: This crystal is used for grounding, protection, cleansing, and integration.

Citrine: It aids with joy, abundance, and the transmutation of energy and serves as an energetic pick-me-up.

"

Life meets us where we are at,
so when we evolve and grow,
we must be willing to assess
what is around us and make
changes necessary to support
our continued transformation.

Self-Awareness

How do we know how to care for ourselves if we are not aware of our needs? How do we know what action to take or changes to make if we do not know what we prefer or how we are affected in certain circumstances? Self-awareness is mindfulness. The more self-aware we are, the more connected we are to our purpose, emotions, intentions, and values. Our capacity to be regularly aware of our state of mind is heavily dependent on our unhealed wounds and our emotional and physical condition. Not only can self-awareness be obscure; it can also be an unpleasant process. Have you ever become aware of one of your deeply rooted survival patterns forged through trauma then begun to see its damaging effects on others? Ouch!

Empaths, like all humans, are complicated and can hurt others. Self-awareness is critical to living an emotionally harmonious life that serves them and those around them. If they are not self-aware, they are not entirely authentic. Everything is affected by their level of self-awareness. Their self-awareness level directly correlates to their ability to thrive professionally, grow in their relationships, and feel confident and fulfilled in their lives.

INNER CIRCLE ASSESSMENT

Energy attracts like energy. Have you ever started your morning out on the wrong foot and, by 1 p.m., had a pileup of adverse events and correlating thoughts that matched the theme of your morning? Life meets us where we are at, so when we evolve and grow, we must be willing to assess what is around us and make the changes necessary to support our continued transformation. Do you have people in your life that are not capable of allowing your perspective? Do you tolerate friends who aren't comfortable with your growth and make attempts to sabotage you?

Yes, any behavior we have that stems from unhealed trauma, low self-esteem, or codependence will be hurtful to others; but others' pain is not an excuse to allow the behavior to go unchecked. Empaths are not responsible for helping them see their pain or even healing them; that is their job. Empaths are responsible for setting boundaries or walking away to protect their own peace and well-being. Remember, mastering one's energy means holding yourself accountable for its care, protection, and maintenance.

Carrying the weight of your and everyone else's emotions, fears, and worries is impossible while maintaining a healthy existence. Nurturing their energy is something empaths should take very seriously. When you begin to create clear boundaries around your energy and prioritize your well-being with nonnegotiable self-care, you will notice an immediate change in the people and situations you draw into your life. To become a true nurturer of your energy means you are willing to claim your energy independence and call your power back to protect yourself and be accountable for how you feel. You are the answer you have been waiting for. What are you waiting for? Have fun, get creative, and allow yourself to experiment. You are deserving of all you desire.

Protect Your Energy Visualization

Find a quiet place to sit where you will not be interrupted. Sit or lay down in a comfortable position, and take five deep cleansing breaths, in through your nose and out through your mouth. On each exhale, focus on relaxing each larger area of your body: head, shoulders, back, buttocks, legs.

Next, set a clear intention. For example: "My intention is for a shield of divine light to drape my body with love, wisdom, and protection. Source's pure light will shield me from any energy vibrating lower than love and allow any lower energies I hold to release." Now imagine a bright, beautiful cobalt blue light ascending from the heavens into the room surrounding your entire body with light.

Take a few deep breaths. On each inhale, imagine the cobalt light entering your lungs and filling your body. On each exhale, see the air exiting your body as a gray or black smoke as the heavier energy escapes.

Take two more deep breaths. This time, see and feel yourself inhaling the feeling of love from the energy around you; and on the exhale, breathe out love to the world.

Set an intention, allowing this shield of light to accept love as it also allows you to give love freely.

Take a few moments and hold your attention on the bright blue light surrounding your body. Sense how this light feels. Sit with the feeling of protection for a few minutes.

Open your eyes.

ch 9 INTUITION

Intuition is that sensation in your gut when you know something is not right.

Or it is that moment when you realized a person is trustworthy without really knowing them. You do not understand why or have evidence for feeling that way—you just know. Intuition is not rational. It does not come after thoughtful consideration or weighing the choices with friends. Intuition is a deep-seated knowing that appears out of nowhere. The process feels unforced and innate. Although intuition is natural to us all, its accuracy can be affected by our experiences and how our subconscious brain processes the situation related to our experiences. In short, sometimes our intuition is spot-on; and sometimes it is not.

If intuition is not logic, can't be seen, and is unexplainable, is it real? The fact that individuals can make clear, sure decisions without analytical thought has intrigued philosophers and scientists for centuries. Although talk of intuition and being intuitive has been the subject for years among "New Age" circles, intuition is also a hot topic in psychology and scientific research.

Various researchers address the validity of intuition and share its importance in our decision-making process. The single most challenging issue with researching intuition, though, is that we cannot witness someone's thought processes. Even with all the advanced brain imaging available, we still cannot observe the process of someone thinking their thoughts. Although scientific evidence lags on intuition, there is still one thing we all agree on: Intuition is real. Science isn't required to convince us that an unknown force guides us from time to time; experiencing is proof.

"

Science isn't required to convince us that an unknown force guides us from time to time; experiencing is proof.

Types of Intuition

All humans have intuition, but not all of us access our intuitive guidance in the same way. There are diverse ways our intuition can nudge us. While I may experience my intuition one way, you may have an intuitive sense that shows up differently than mine. Daily practice can strengthen intuition, just like regular exercise can build up muscle. If you want to connect to your intuition more deeply, you need to under-stand how it interacts with you, get familiar with how your higher self speaks through you, and take the empowering step of letting it guide you. There are different ways our inner voice speaks to us. Below you will find four methods intuition uses to get our attention.

- ***Clairsentience (feeling):*** This type of intuition is a popular one for empaths and one many of us do not realize we are experiencing. Clairsentience is feeling things in our bodies that are not always ours. It permits us to notice feelings that furnish us with information about our surroundings. Is this my sadness? Is this my anger? Is this my fear? These questions became a staple in my day-to-day life when it became clear that my intuition appeared to me through clairsentience.

- ***Clairvoyance (seeing):*** This type of intuition is one that Hollywood got a hold of years ago and one it uses in all sorts of fabricated stories. Clairvoyance sees things in unconventional ways that defy reasoning. It is the ability to receive messages through imagery, comparisons, and seeing the invisible like spirits or energy.

- ***Clairaudience (hearing):*** Clairaudience is the hearing of messages and guidance in our minds apart from our judgmental mind. Years ago, there was a big unexpect-ed and yet-to-arrive snowstorm. The state was not ready, the meteorologists were unfazed, and the governor was in denial and had not ordered the roads' treatment. I called my children's school asking if any kids had gone home early. The staff told me no and that they were not concerned about a potential storm. I hung up the phone, and a voice said, "Go get your children." Within the first five minutes of the drive, the skies opened, and I was driving ten miles per hour (16 km/h) in a blizzard. My children were home safe that evening while other children slept in school gyms and on buses stranded on the highways. My guiding voice defied logic that day.

• *Claircognizance (knowing):* Have you ever known something without rational reason and logic was not part of the process—you just know? Your ability to "just know" was your claircognizance intuition. Many of us ignore this guidance and allow others to talk us out of it. Claircognizance has been called the "mother's instinct" or a gut feeling. Has claircognizance ever told you something was not right or nudged you to buy a stock and you did not listen? Then I bet you have experienced "ignored intuition regret" and said things like "I knew I shouldn't have or should have done that." Ugh!

Empaths and Intuition

Of all the gifts empaths have, powerful intuition is one of my favorites. Empaths are like supercharged data processors; they have access to all sorts of data, including a personal line to higher guidance. When they create a lifestyle that prioritizes their well-being, including moments of stillness, they open themselves to the specific messages meant to guide them in every moment. Since childhood, I have known about the concept of intuition but had not grasped its importance or its presence in my life until much later.

From an early age, well into my thirties, I had little to no trust in myself, my body, or my ability to withstand what I felt. For decades, I was fully vested in the outside world, allowing it to tell me who I was and show me what to do. I detached from trusting myself; therefore, I disconnected from acknowledging my intuition and following it. During those years of disconnection, I cursed the lack of guidance I received. I was convinced God had left me to fend for myself. Looking back, I see that my intuition was guiding me the entire time; but I chose to ignore it and instead follow other people's feelings and energy. Each time I decided to ignore my intuition to "keep the peace" or "be accepted," I wound up in more pain and anguish. I used the pain as proof that God abandoned me, not that I discarded the guidance.

Years ago, while navigating the darkest elements of my spiritual awakening, my inner guidance was more precise than I had ever experienced. My intuition guided me to make self-trust a priority. As I started to change how I lived, making self-care nonnegotiable, I began awakening to my real strengths and purpose. The more I believed in my power, the more comfortable I was with trusting my inner guidance and taking leaps of faith. The journey back to myself has been one of separating from what others feel and reconnecting to how I feel. I learned young that others' feelings and emotions were powerful, and to cope, I prioritized their needs over mine. Looking back, I see that the moments of reprieve I wished for in choosing their needs over mine were quick and temporary; but the effects on my self-trust and self-worth were long-lasting and devastating.

An empath's intuition is one of their best assets, and reconnecting to it can alter the trajectory of their lives. When empaths trust themselves, they open to unlimited possibilities and experiencing the life they were born to live.

Some remarkable benefits of prioritizing intuition are as follows:

Heightened creativity: Recognizing deeper truths, patterns, and symbolism in your life opens communication between your conscious and unconscious minds, allowing for increased creative flow and expression.

Enhanced self-awareness: As you learn to recognize and trust your intuition, you will begin realizing your authentic desires and increasing the speed at which you discover things about your true self.

Efficient decision making: When you trust your intuition, you make decisions more quickly; and the choices you make are sounder and of more benefit to us.

Renewed mental well-being: Establishing your connection to your intuition requires prioritizing stillness and awareness, and I have discussed the positive benefits of meditation. An increase in self-trust also elevates self-worth and happiness.

Elimination of negative forces in your life: When you begin to trust yourself, you start to see what is best for you and feel confident in letting go of people, places, and things that are not. This act alone can have an incredible impact on your life.

Deeper connection to your body: Many empaths, including myself, disconnect from their bodies, hoping to limit what they feel. Their body is the conduit of all they feel and perceive, and reestablishing the relationship with their inner guidance means realizing the gift that is their body.

Alignment with your purpose: Intuition is the voice of your soul, and when you listen to that voice, you align yourself with your highest purpose in every moment.

Knowing when to say no: When I first began to follow my soul, my favorite saying was "I'm not being guided to do that." Prioritizing my higher voice meant I could make an empowered decision based on my feelings, not their reactions. Remember, you connect the dots of following your intuition in hindsight. You must be willing to take the step forward, and confidence grows within you.

Intuition is essential for enhanced prosperity, and in all of us, we also have free will—we get to choose whether we follow it. After years of ignoring it, choosing to follow it can feel scary. In the beginning, I fumbled through doubt and followed my fear a few times but eventually became more comfortable bypassing my mind and staying in my heart. As I did, my confidence grew; and proof that something incredible was happening appeared. The more I followed my inner guidance, the stronger my intuition became; and it all began with a leap of faith (and a powerful desire to live life differently).

Trusting Our Bodies

A common belief marked on us after trauma, abuse, or prolonged emotional overload is that we are not safe in our bodies. When we continually feel physically, emotionally, or verbally threatened, we may embrace the idea that our body is not trustworthy and choose to escape our body to live in our distractible mind. For as long as I can remember, I viewed my body as a misery source, not a refuge. I learned at an early age that avoiding the full spectrum of emotions around me required separating from my body. Many young empaths and highly sensitive children do not understand their heightened sensory experience and lack the tools to navigate it. The emotions, feelings, and energy they observe radiate through their bodies without guidance or understanding. Over time, they begin to fear what their bodies feel and assume they have no control over their experience. They then start disconnecting from their bodies in hopes to avoid their intense senses.

Developing your intuition requires a connection to your body because our bodies convey our highest wisdom. Getting accustomed to trusting your body may bring some profound inner challenges. Reconnecting may bring up a lot of emotions at first, and that is normal. Remember to be easy on yourself, go slow, and always know you are responsible and trustworthy for your safety. Tips for reconnecting to your body include the following:

• **Be still and notice.** To start, do this for ten minutes a few days a week—quietly sit where you will not be interrupted. Take this time to notice. Notice your feet in your shoes and the breeze touching your skin. Notice how your upper back feels. Notice your breath and your ears. Notice how it all feels. The intention is to notice.

• **Verbalize it.** When your body begins to feel fear, anger, or sadness, take a moment to verbalize what that feeling feels like in your body. For example, "I am feeling anxious; it feels like constriction and heaviness in my upper chest. If this feeling could talk, it would say, 'I don't have enough time to get this project completed. I'm going to fail.'" When you can verbalize your feelings, you assess the untruth under the feeling, allowing you to soothe yourself.

- **Address your trauma.** When you heal what holds you apart from your body, you will naturally begin to move back toward yourself. I found EMDR (eye movement desensitization and reprocessing) to be a beneficial treatment when I was progressing through the darkest parts.

- **Create.** Add some creativity to your life. Bring your body and mind together to write, draw, paint, sing, or design. Creativity is proven to increase happiness, improve mental health, boost immune function, and enhance cognitive function.

- **Move.** Movement of all sorts, when paired with body awareness, elevates connection. The caveat is enjoying how you move. Turn the music up and dance; find your favorite park and walk. When you move, can you stay conscious of your body? Try mindful walking. With each step, feel your feet stepping onto the pavement. When dancing, feel your waist as you bend and sway. Move for love of your body, not for hate.

Living in a world that inundates us with body shame messages, makes desire taboo, encourages us to suppress feelings, and preaches mind over body, it is no wonder most of us left our bodies years ago. Being connected to our bodies is vital for our mental and physical health. The mind-body connection allows us to feel the joy and purpose of our lives, others' happiness, and the planet's beauty. We deserve to feel good. Reclaiming our birthright to occupy our bodies fully will transform our thoughts, emotions, and relationships.

Intuition vs. Fear

An exciting opportunity has presented itself to you. Is it the right move, or is it a distraction from your actual path? When met with a chance to expand, it is natural to feel uncertain and reluctant; and sometimes our mind's voice can be misleading and convince us it is intuition. So, how do we know if the inner guidance we receive is fear or intuition? Knowing our fear from our intuition is an important distinction to make. My fear has led me all over the place, and each time I end up worse off than I began. An opportunity would present itself. I would jump, thinking the excitement was my intuition when, instead, it was my ego aching to feel worthy in the eyes of others. Or I would say no, assuming a natural fear of growth was intuition steering me away.

Everything is energy, even words; and our body, if we pay attention, has a sensation when truth moves through it. A statement rooted in truth or yes will feel a specific way in your body, and information embedded with untruth or no will feel another way. In my body, truth feels open and light and resonates in my upper chest and throat. A no feels dense and heavy and has a slight twinge in my upper chest and throat. Connecting back to our body allows us to feel into our decision and differentiate between our fear misleading us and our intuition guiding us.

Following are a few things I do when I need clarity:

- I remind myself that my inner wisdom lives in my body, not in my thoughts.

- I communicate with all involved that I will "sleep on it," giving myself time to connect to my body for clarity.

- I take a full moment of stillness (this could be five minutes or twenty), however long I need, to calm my mind and quiet my thoughts. Once I reach a calm state, I focus all my attention on my body. I tend to concentrate on the space between my upper chest and belly. Once I am calm and focused, I ask the question, "Is this the right choice for me?" Then I allow my body's intrinsic wisdom to radiate the answer back to me. I feel for it; feeling for it means putting my mind aside. A yes feels light, almost airy in the space between my throat and chest. My mind might try to bring thoughts of excitement into the mix, but I will set that aside. I am engaged in focusing on the subtle light sensations within my body. If it is a sensation of space or light, then it is a yes. If it is dense or heavy with a slight tinge, it is a no.

You can mix up your questions to best suit you. Some alternatives are "Is saying yes the best decision for me?" "Does this feel like growth?" "Do I feel safe saying yes?" Like everything we do, practice makes us better at the task. The wisdom and guidance we are looking for is in our bodies, and with practice, we can strengthen our connection to it.

Tips to Strengthen Intuition

Intuitive guidance is an empath's most valuable resource, and following it brings about countless advantages for them. The more I began pursuing my intuition, the better grounded and safe I felt within my body and feeling my emotions. The connection to my higher truth allowed me to easily discern my feelings from other people's and see when I was making decisions from fear, enabling me to make more empowered decisions. The road back to myself and my body had its difficulties. Still, with consistent focus and effort, I was able to turn my search for answers from outside myself to inside myself, leading to a sense of emotional stability, self-trust, and self-confidence.

Here are five things I incorporated into my life and do every day to strengthen my intuition.

1. **Journal.** Empaths can easily slip into mind mode, so processing their thoughts and emotions is crucial. Journaling not only meets the need to process; it also helps in intuition awareness. When their minds overpower them with busy thoughts, it blocks their ability to sense their intuition's soft subtle nudges. Writing can allow feelings and expression to flow, and without the mind dictating the next move, one can find their intuition stepping in and taking part in the creative process.

2. **Prioritize rest.** This one was a struggle for me at first. One of my go-to trauma responses is overproductivity, meaning it is easy for busyness to take over in hopes of reaching a fabricated and always-changing "good enough" finish line. If the body communicates its inner guidance through sensation, respecting the body's needs seems to be an obvious choice. If we are pushing the body to overwhelm, are we connected and honoring its well-being? Do you believe your body and intuition work better in a cared-for environment or when neglected? Intuition is subtle and soft; we must slow down if we want to notice it. Begin paying attention to your body's cues, pause, assess, then take action to care.

3. **Plan alone time.** I began hearing when I stopped listening. Prioritizing time without others empowers us to start questioning what we believe. It gives us the space to tend to our feelings and emotions and restore the bond with our intuition. In the beginning, I needed a lot of time alone because I had many things to sort through, unlearn, and dismantle. As the connection to my inner voice strengthened, though, I found my perfect balance of immersion and solitude.

4. **Increase body awareness.** The body is where intuition lives. I use meditations specifically for body connection. There are excellent guided meditation options available online, and I included some of my favorites in the Resources section at the end of the book. Taking deep belly breaths is also a tool I use to bring my awareness into my body. Wherever you are, take deep breaths; but when you do, inhale through your nose and allow the air to fill your belly. Placing your right hand over your stomach can assist in staying aware of the air movement.

5. **Follow your gut and say, "Thanks . . . more of that."** There's no better way to begin trusting yourself than leaping, and when you do— and the confirmation comes through that your intuition led you—express tremendous gratitude, clap loudly for yourself, and say, "Yes . . . more of that, please."

"

With consistent focus and
effort, I was able to turn my
search for answers from outside
myself to inside myself, leading
to a sense of emotional stability,
self-trust, and self-confidence.

Intuition Strengthening Exercises

Besides daily habits that help me strengthen and connect with my intuition, I have also turned to fun exercises that make great add-ons to my journaling and build confidence when I feel a need for reassurance.

AUTOMATIC WRITING

1. Grab a piece of paper and pencil, sit down, and quiet your mind by meditating for five to ten minutes.

2. Think about something you would like guidance on, then soften your hand and allow your hand to write as though it were separate from your mind.

3. Try not to overthink and try to let go.

   The more you do this, the better you get at it; and soon your intuition will be flowing through your hand onto paper with guidance that will astound you.

GUESS THE NEXT CARD

1. Get a deck of UNO cards. (We care about the colors.)

2. Shuffle the cards and place them face down in a pile.

3. Clear your mind; meditate, if needed, for five minutes.

4. Pick up the deck of cards. Hold the cards facedown in your hand.

5. Guess the color of each top card. Keep flipping; feel for the right new answer.

6. Place the cards you get right in one pile and those you do not get right in another.

   Remember, intuition is calm, clear, and quick. This exercise was a game-changer for my intuition confidence.

NOTICE EVERYTHING GAME

Most of us walk around completely unaware of what is going on around us. Things happen, and we do not even notice—like the time I turned to go to my daughter's school when I was headed to the grocery store. Our intuition gives us subtle signs and messages, and it can be easy for them to float on by unrecognized. The more we notice everything—from the color and texture of the fabric to the sound of the train in the distance—the more conscious we become of inner wisdom.

Intuition requires presence. Practice being aware in the present moment. We can do this by observing how things look, sound, smell, and feel all around us.

THE MESSAGES

Before you start your day or when you are looking for clarification, ask your inner guru to send you a message. You get to choose your preferred method, but most times, the wisdom comes where it is easiest for us to notice. Mine often come in books and songs. I will ask for guidance, then open a book—any book I am guided to—and turn it to a specific page, and then a particular paragraph on that page. I then allow that paragraph to be my guide.

You can also do this with music. For example, set the intention that the next song you hear will contain the guidance you need. And then pay attention! The signs will most certainly come through.

Intuition is our innate ability to know when something is not right. It is like our own navigation system advising us to take the next left or at the next exit make a U-turn. Trusting the guidance leads us toward the highest vision of ourselves, our greatest joy, and our deepest desires. Empaths are like super antennas with the ability to pick up and process all sorts of subtleties. When they pair that with intuition, their decision making becomes a superpower. The combination of our sensitivity and intuition allows us to put our finely tuned nervous system to work and thrive in the face of adversity.

Empath, you are perfectly made. Your ability to notice every detail gives you a potential advantage; whether you nurture yourself and tap into that advantage is up to you. Trust that the higher guidance you are searching for is available to you, and with the dedication to practice, self-care, nourishment, and healing, you can unlock the fullest expression of your soul.

AFTERWORD—STEPPING INTO YOUR POWER

To be in your power means you are in alignment,

that the focus of everything you do is on the same goal serving a similar purpose. What is your highest intention? Do you sense your greater purpose?

I want to feel my power by remembering and experiencing the highest truth in every moment, meaning, amid diversity and calm, I want to realize my capacity as a spiritual being in human form. I want my inner wisdom to drown out the fear around me and lead me to embody and feel myself as love. I want to feel my potential. Because empaths can sense and feel others' suffering, many of them believe it is their responsibility to carry and soothe the weight of the world. But the weight is not theirs to bear; it never was.

They are not here to save the world. In fact, the impact they can make rests solely on their ability to show up as their whole authentic selves, modeling what it looks like to take 100 percent responsibility for their well-being.

By embracing the empathic soul's needs, prioritizing self-care, and healing, we automatically step into our full potential, which naturally supports others in stepping into their power.

The journey of an empath stepping into their power is not about what they can do and be for others but how well they turn their gifts toward themselves and be the radiant light they were born to be. By focusing on caring for themselves, they personify the energy of healing and love; and with a soul untethered by fear, they can change the energy in any room just by being themselves. I invite you to join me; we are on this journey together. Where you are on the path is not relevant, but your willingness to take the initial step and keep moving is essential.

Survival is where we start. It is the place where we struggle to get through the day. We beg and plead for the energy around us to change and for the people around us to change. Survival is where my mental and physical health crashed, including my adrenals. We do not have the knowledge or tools to understand or care for our sensitive nature. We highly depend on survival mechanisms and distractions to get us through the day. We suffer a lot in survival, and many of us settle upon the false belief that we are fundamentally flawed.

Next is the crossroad. As I entered this phase, I hit a wall. I remember thinking to myself, "If something doesn't drastically change, I won't survive." This was the start of a dramatic shift. The crossroad can look and feel differently for everyone, and it does not always come with a sense of relief. But in the foundation of this crossroad is an intuitive glimmer of hope. You do not know how it will happen, and overcoming the feelings of despair will be a challenge, but deep inside you, you sense a greater plan for yourself. We begin to look in various places for answers. Our inner rebel emerges, and we start questioning what people throughout our lives told us to believe.

Then comes accountability. Accountability is a stage many of us resist. To embrace responsibility means we have healed enough to step away from victimhood and reach a level of acceptance, putting us in charge of our energy and experiences.

Please hear me when I say that we are not responsible for the initial events that traumatize us, but we hold power as to whether past events continue to hurt us. Accountability also means seeing how our pain manifests into behaviors that hurt others, and this can be a tough one for a sensitive soul to navigate. Seeking support is an excellent option during this time. In this portion of the journey, we begin to feel encouraged and committed to our self-care. We start to experiment with boundaries, journaling, nature, grounding, reading all that we can about energy, and identifying our unique needs. During this phase, you may notice that those around you are growing more uncomfortable while you are becoming more comfortable. When we prioritize ourselves, it disrupts relationships that benefited from us prioritizing their well-being over ours. Remind yourself that you are safe and loved and that through caring for yourself first, we pave the way for others to do the same. This is when we begin valuing, protecting, and nourishing our energy. This is the stage where we start to turn inward for answers instead of pointing our fingers outward.

Finally, there's stepping into our power. When we step into our power, our self-care has become nonnegotiable. It is as habitual as brushing our teeth. We fully embrace ourselves as a highly sensitive, empathic, unique, feeling soul and no longer subscribe to living like the rest of the world. We know how long we can attend a party without feeling drained, we understand the effect on our energy when certain people visit, and we act before, during, and after to tend to ourselves without guilt. We accept ourselves, honor our needs, and stand up for ourselves. Like life, this stage is not without darkness. But now, instead of feeling swallowed by the dark, you use it as a guide for more profound healing. Instead of hiding, you double down on self-care and ride the wave of growth. By staying centered and grounded, you begin removing your obstacles and freely sharing your gifts to benefit others worldwide.

Empath, you are a vital piece of the puzzle.

You are filled with the secrets of the universe.

You are aware of more than is seen, and
at times your voice seems lost.

But on the surface, you have the power
to change it all.

You are unique, but you are free.

You are sensitive, but you are powerful.

You feel immense pain, but you feel
overwhelming joy.

Show them how to live in the now.

Demonstrate what it means to move
energy with stillness.

Show them how to live in the light with
the presence of darkness.

Your essence is LOVE. Embrace that.

Resources

Books

The Alchemist by Paulo Coelho

The Big Leap by Gay Hendricks

Breaking the Habit of Being Yourself by Dr. Joe Dispenza

A Course in Miracles by Helen Schucman

The Empath's Survival Guide: Life Strategies for Sensitive People by Judith Orloff, M.D.

Energetic Boundaries by Cyndi Dale

The Highly Sensitive Person by Elaine N. Aron, Ph.D.

The Power of Now by Eckhart Tolle

The Power of Vulnerability by Brené Brown, Ph.D.

StrengthsFinder 2.0 by Tom Rath

The War of Art by Steven Pressfield

Meditations

Grounding guided meditation: www.realizedempath.com/grounding-meditation

Letting go guided meditation: www.realizedempath.com/empath-letting-go-meditation

Body awareness meditation: www.youtube.com/watch?v=T0nuKBVQS7M

Energy-cleansing meditation: www.youtube.com/watch?v=awL9KlYhTtU

Healing binaural beat meditation: www.youtube.com/watch?v=hdmvMc7TZn0

Websites

www.acestoohigh.com Visit website to calculate your Adverse Childhood Experience score.

Centers for Disease Control and Prevention. "Violence Prevention." www.cdc.gov/violenceprevention/aces/

Articles

Acevedo, Bianca, Elaine Aron, Sarah Pospos, and Dana Jessen. "The Functional Highly Sensitive Brain: A Review of the Brain Circuits Underlying Sensory Processing Sensitivity and Related Disorders." *Philosophical Transactions of the Royal Society B: Biological Sciences* 373, no. 1744 (2018): 20170161. doi:10.1098/rstb.2017.0161.

American Psychological Association. "Building Your Resilience." www.apa.org/topics/resilience/. February 1, 2020.

Brackett, Marc A., Susan E. Rivers, Sara Shiffman, Nicole Lerner, and Peter Salovey. "Relating Emotional Abilities to Social Functioning: A Comparison of Self-Report and Performance Measures of Emotional Intelligence." *Journal of Personality and Social Psychology* 91, no. 4 (2006): 780–95. doi:10.1037/0022-3514.91.4.780.

Catama, Bryan V., Alayla Louise A. Del Castillo, Athena Grace S. Espino, Melanie K. Beleo, Leda Mae V. Blanca, Moira Angela B. Bunagan, and Eliel Dhenise M. Cruz. "Adventitious Blindness: The Road to Self-Acceptance." *International Journal of Research Studies in Psychology* 6, no. 2 (2017): 85–102. doi:10.5861/ijrsp.2017.1844.

Corso, Phaedra S., Valerie J. Edwards, Xiangming Fang, and James A. Mercy. "Health-Related Quality of Life among Adults Who Experienced Maltreatment during Childhood." *American Journal of Public Health* 98 (2008): 1094–1100. doi:10.2105/AJPH.2007.119826.

Dear, Greg E., Clare M. Roberts, and Lois Lange. "Defining Codependency: A Thematic Analysis of Published Definitions." In *Advances in Psychology Research*, edited by Serge P. Shohov, 34: 189–205. New York: Nova Science Publishers, 2004.

Eurich, Tasha. "What Self-Awareness Really Is (and How to Cultivate It)." *Harvard Business Review*. January 4, 2018. https://hbr.org/2018/01/what-self-awareness-really-is-and-how-to-cultivate-it.

Freud, Sigmund. "Further Remarks on the Neuro-psychoses of Defence." Standard Edition 3 (1896): 157–85.

Freud, Sigmund. "The Neuro-psychoses of Defence." *Standard Edition* 3 (1894): 41–61. Lepore, Stephen J. "Expressive Writing Moderates the Relation between Intrusive Thoughts and Depressive Symptoms." *Journal of Personality and Social Psychology* 73, no. 5 (1997): 1030–7. doi:10.1037/0022-3514.73.5.1030.

MacLachlan, Alice. "Unreasonable Resentments." *Journal of Social Philosophy* 41 (2010): 422–41.

Malle, Bertram F., Steve Guglielmo, and Andrew E. Monroe. "A Theory of Blame." *Psychological Inquiry* 25, no. 2 (2014): 147–86. doi:10.1080/1047840X.2014.877340.

Ming Zhang, Mohamed Moalin, Lily Vervoort, Zheng Wen Li, Wen Bo Wu, and Guido Haenen. "Connecting Western and Eastern Medicine from an Energy Perspective." *International Journal of Molecular Sciences* 20, no. 6 (2019): 1512. doi:10.3390/ijms20061512.

Öllinger, Michael, and Albrecht von Müller. "Search and Coherence-Building in Intuition and Insight Problem Solving." *Frontiers in Psychology* 8 (2017): 827. doi:10.3389/fpsyg.2017.00827.

Pretz, Jean E., Jeffrey B. Brookings, Lauren A. Carlson, Tamera Keiter Humbert, Michael Roy, Meghan Jones, and Daniel Memmert. "Development and Validation of a New Measure of Intuition: The Types of Intuition Scale." *Journal of Behavioral Decision Making* 27, no. 5 (2014): 454–67. doi:10.1002/bdm.182027.10.1002/.1820.

Ranganathan, Vinoth K., Vlodek Siemionow, Jing Z. Liu, Vinod Sahgal, and Guang H. Yue. "From Mental Power to Muscle Power—Gaining Strength by Using the Mind." *Neuropsychologia* 42, no. 7 (2004): 944-–56. doi:10.1016/j.neuropsychologia.2003.11.018.

Sobkow, Agata, Jakub Traczyk, Scott Barry Kaufman, and Czeslaw Nosal. "The Structure of Intuitive Abilities and Their Relationships with Intelligence and Openness to Experience." *Intelligence* 67 (2018): 1–10. doi:10.1016/j.intell.2017.12.001.

Tangney, June P., and Ronda L. Dearing. *Shame and Guilt.* New York: Guilford Press, 2002.

Truax, Charles B., and Robert R. Carkhuff. *Toward Effective Counseling and Psychotherapy: Training and Practice.* New York: Aldine, 1967.

University of Cambridge. "Genes Play a Role in Empathy." *ScienceDaily*, March 12, 2018.

Weir, Kirsten. "The Exercise Effect." *Monitor on Psychology* 42, no. 11 (2011): 48–51. www.apa.org/monitor/2011/12/exercise.

Wild, Jennifer. "Is Bullying Worse Than Child Abuse When It Comes to Mental Health?" *The Conversation.* April 29, 2015. https://theconversation.com/is-bullying-worse-than-child-abuse-when-it-comes-to-mental-health-40872.

ABOUT
THE AUTHOR

Kristen Schwartz, MA, CTRC, is a writer, entrepreneur, attuned empathic healer, and certified trauma recovery coach.

She holds a bachelor's degree in psychology and a master's degree in counseling. In 2016, fueled by passion and recognizing the need for empaths and highly sensitive people to realize their potential, Kristen became the founder of Realized Empath. Within this wellness community, empaths unite for support, inspiration, and healing. Join the fun at www.realizedempath.com.

When she's not deep diving with other empaths, Kristen is planning her next travel adventure or reading a book in a hammock amongst the trees. Kristen resides in Georgia with her husband and two children.